No part of this publication may be reproduced, transmitted, translated or stored without the express written permission of the publisher. Created and printed in the United States of America.

LIMIT OF LIABILITY/DISCLAIMER OF WARRANTY: THE PUBLISHER AND THE AUTHOR MAKE NO REPRESENTATIONS OR WARRANTIES WITH RESPECT TO THE ACCURACY OR COMPLETENESS OF THE CONTENTS OF THIS WORK AND SPECIFICALLY DISCLAIM ALL WARRANTIES, INCLUDING WITHOUT LIMITATION WARRANTIES OF FITNESS FOR A PARTICULAR PURPOSE. NO WARRANTY MAY BE CREATED OR EXTENDED BY SALES OR PROMOTIONAL MATERIALS. THE ADVICE AND STRATEGIES CONTAINED HEREIN MAY NOT BE SUITABLE FOR EVERY SITUATION. THIS WORK IS SOLD WITH THE UNDERSTANDING THAT THE PUBLISHER IS NOT ENGAGED IN RENDERING LEGAL, ACCOUNTING, OR OTHER PROFESSIONAL SERVICES. IF PROFESSIONAL ASSISTANCE IS REQUIRED, THE SERVICE OF A COMPETENT PROFESSIONAL PERSON SHOULD BE SOUGHT. NEITHER THE PUBLISHER NOR THE AUTHOR SHALL BE LIABLE FOR DAMAGES ARISING HEREFROM. THE FACT THAT AN ORGANIZATION OR WEBSITE IS REFERRED TO IN THIS WORK AS A CITATION AND/OR A POTENTIAL SOURCE OF FURTHER INFORMATION DOES NOT MEAN THAT THE AUTHOR OR THE PUBLISHER ENDORSES THE INFORMATION THE ORGANIZATION OR WEBSITE MAY PROVIDE OR RECOMMENDATIONS IT MAY MAKE. FURTHER, READERS SHOULD BE AWARE THAT INTERNET WEBSITES LISTED IN THIS WORK MAY HAVE CHANGED OR DISAPPEARED BETWEEN WHEN THIS WORK WAS WRITTEN AND WHEN IT WAS READ.

Feb. 2013

Preface

The Hands-on Microsoft Office Excel 2007 Basic Training manual will provide the reader a jump-start on learning how to use Excel. Individuals who learn best by doing, will reap benefits from this manual. This manual contains illustrated examples and step-by-step instructions which cover such topics as the ribbon interface, data tables, PivotTables, PivotCharts, formulas and printing.

The intent of this manual is to provide the reader several basic real world organizational problems that can be solved through the use of MS Office Excel 2007. The reader will learn the basic features of Microsoft Office Excel 2007 by solving these problems. To enhance the learning process, a CD is included that contains the solutions for the organizational problems presented in this manual.

Table of Contents

1. **Introduction**…….5

2. **The Start and Finish Lines** - The Office ICON Menu: Open, Create, Save , Print and more……..8

3. **Tab your way to productivity** - The Ribbon Interface……………………………………………………15

4. **Creating a Spreadsheet (Let there be data)** – Columns and Rows…Columns and Rows……….25

5. **Creating a Data Table** – One record at a time………………………………………………………………….47

6. **Making Sense** - PivotTables: Summarizing Results and Data Analysis)………………………….59

7. **A picture is worth a thousand words** - Charts and Graphs (Trends in Data)………………………85

8. **Looks are everything** – Formatting and Themes ……………………………………………………..101

9. **The finished product** - Printing: Headers , Footers, Preview , Page Breaks………………………111

Introduction: What is a Spreadsheet?

Introduction
Module 1

Collins Dictionary Definitions

Spreadsheet noun
a computer program that allows easy entry and manipulation
of figures, equations, and text, used especially for financial planning and budgeting.

DATA

Introduction
Module 1

Components of Excel Workbook

This course will explore the basic features of three components of Microsoft Excel 2007.

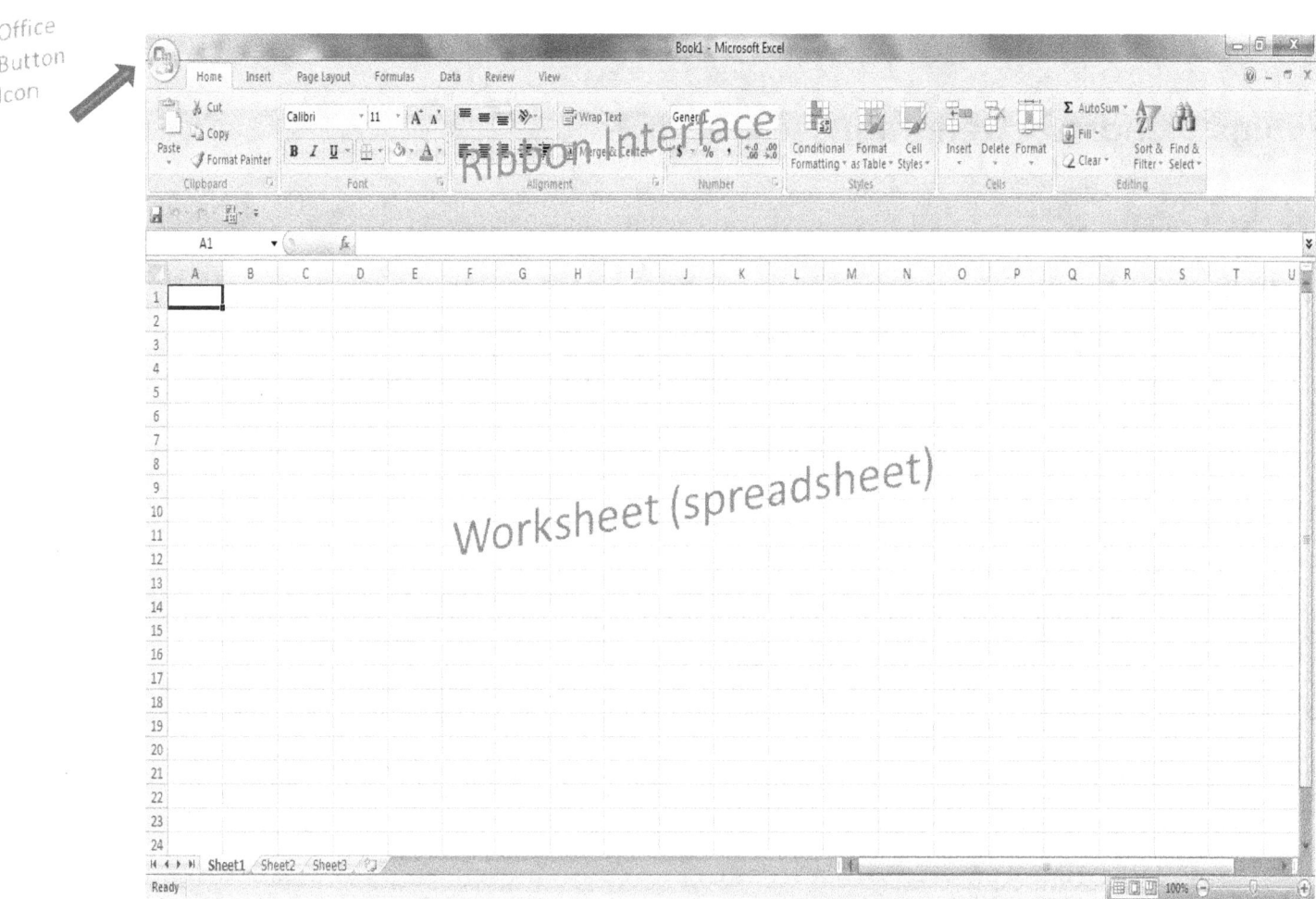

Figure 1-1 Three component of MS Excel 2007.

- Office Button Icon
- Ribbon Interface
- Worksheet

Icon Menu

Module 2

THE OFFICE BUTTON ICON MENU
THE START AND FINISH LINES

Icon Menu
Module 2

To initiate Excel, select the Microsoft Office Excel 2007 application from your MS Windows start menu or MS Windows desktop. A new spreadsheet will be presented. In the top left corner of the spreadsheet you will see the Office Icon Button.

The **Office Button** icon, is where you will begin. It contains the file management functions.

As you can see, in **figure 2-1**, the "Office Button" icon menu is divided into 3 sections. To access, the functions, within the "Office Button" menu, click once on the icon.

We will informally call the 3 sections:

       1) File Handling (create, open or save).
    2) File Print and Publish (print, prepare, send and publish).
    3) File Close (exit).

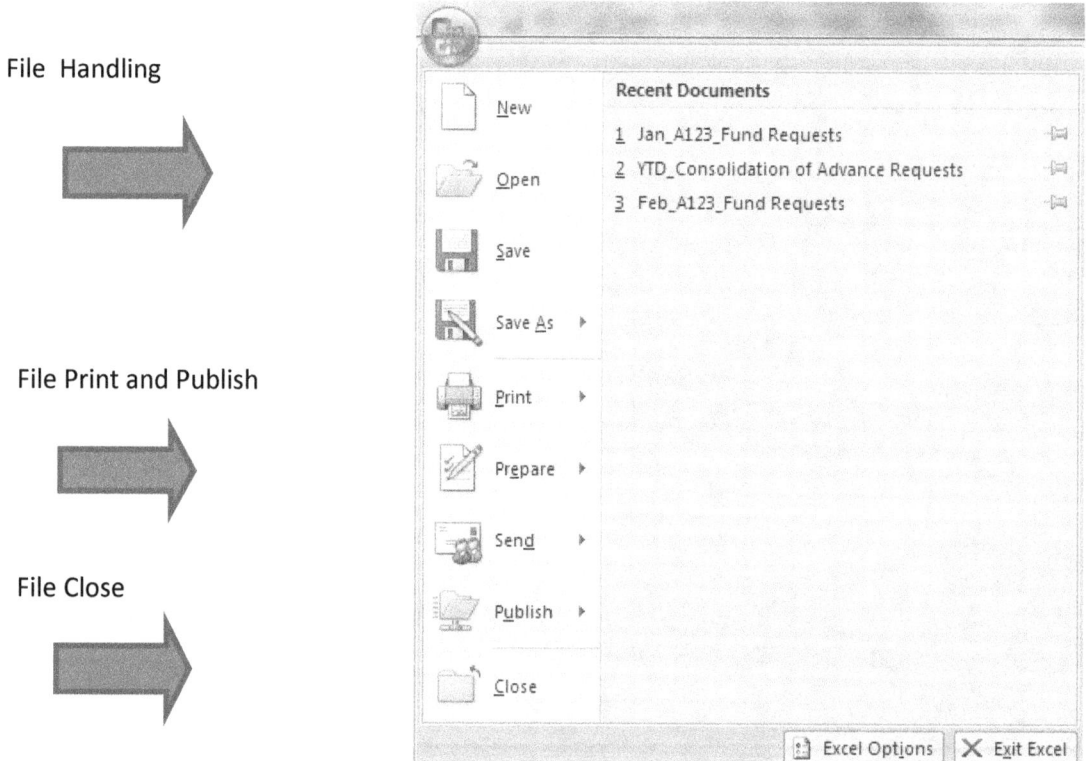

Figure 2-1 Office Button menu file management commands.

TopToolsandTraining LLC

1) **File Handling** (create, open or save).
   To create a spreadsheet, the "New" icon should be selected.
   To access an existing spreadsheet, select the "Open" icon.
   To save a copy of your spreadsheet to a storage destination (disk, hard drive, thumbdrive, etc.), select the "Save" icon.
   To save an updated spreadsheet to another location or give it another name, select "Save As".

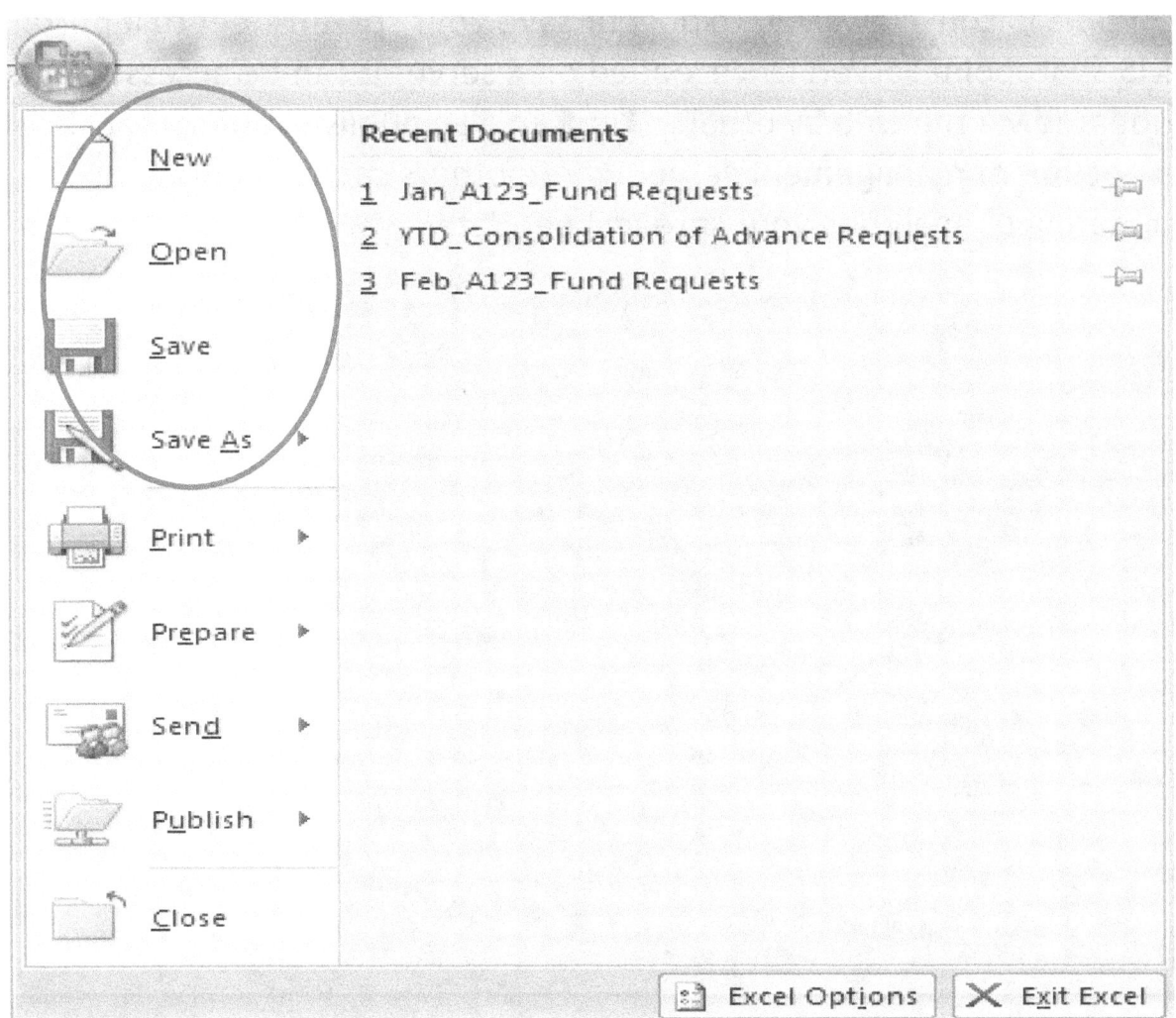

Figure 2-2 Office Button menu's file handling commands.

Icon Menu
Module 2

2) Print and Publish (print, prepare, send and publish) **(figure 2-3).**

> ➢ **Print** icon allows you to print all or part of your spreadsheet, so it can be used in a presentation or report.

> ➢ **Prepare** icon allows you to finalize your spreadsheet by adding encryptions, titles, signatures, and more.

> ➢ **Send** icon allows you to send a copy of your spreadsheet as an email, Acrobat pdf, or fax.

> ➢ **Publish** icon allows you to post or save your spreadsheet to a portal or MS Sharepoint server. Once loaded on a server it can be accessed and updated via the web by others. You can also publish your spreadsheet to a document management server where others can collaborate by updating or analyzing your spreadsheet data.

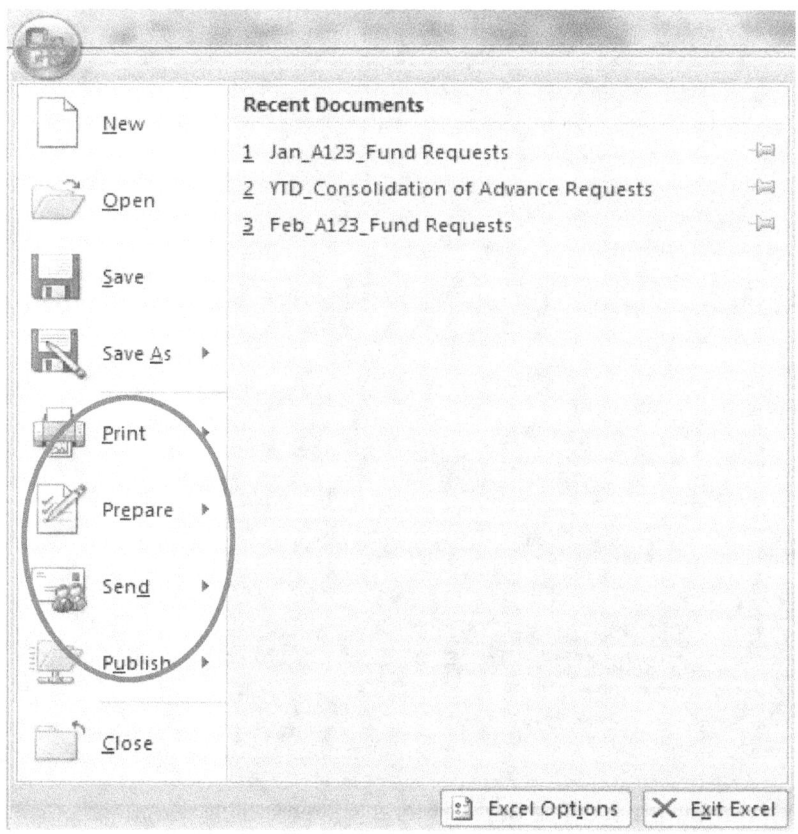

Figure 2-3 Office Button menu 's file print and publishing commands.

TopToolsandTraining LLC

3) Close (Exit gracefully)

The "Close" icon will allow you to properly exit your new or updated spreadsheet. When you are done working on your spreadsheet, choosing the "Close" icon will cause Excel to display a prompt menu. The menu will ask, "Do you want to save changes you made?". It is a good practice to always select the "Close" icon before shutting down the Excel program.

Figure 2-4 Office Button menu 's file close command.

Icon Menu
Module 2

The "Office Button" icon menu is also the place where you will find a list of your most recently updated documents. This list serves as a reminder of where you left off. MS Excel provides you the option to permanently pin a document to this list. Once pinned, the pinned document will always be present on your "Recent Documents" list. To pin a document place the cursor on the pin icon located to the far right of the document name you want to pin. Next, click the left mouse button once. In our example, figure 2-6, the "Test workbook 3" document was pinned.

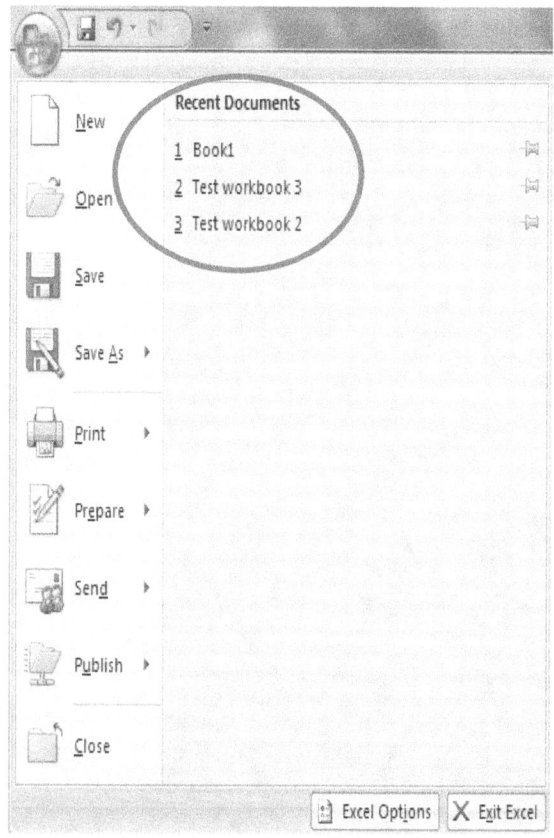

Figure 2-5 Office Button menu **before** pinning "Test workbook 3" document.

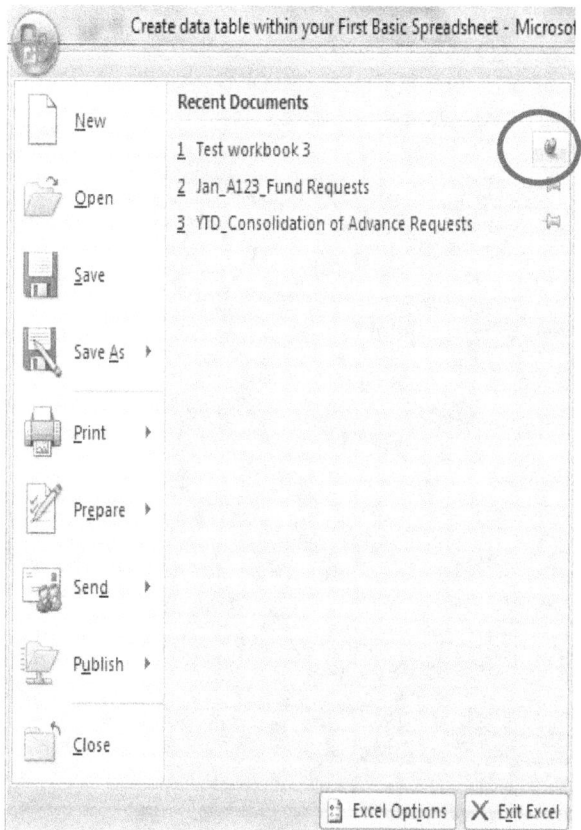

Figure 2-6 Office Button menu **after** pinning "Test workbook 3" document.

What have you learned so far?

1) How to create, open and save a spreadsheet.
2) How to print, prepare, send and publish a spreadsheet.
3) How to close a spreadsheet.

THE RIBBON INTERFACE
TAB YOUR WAY TO PRODUCTIVITY

The seven basic tabs within the Ribbon Interface.

Figure 3-1 MS Office Excel 2007 Ribbon Interface tabs.

The Home tab

Ribbon Interface
Module 3

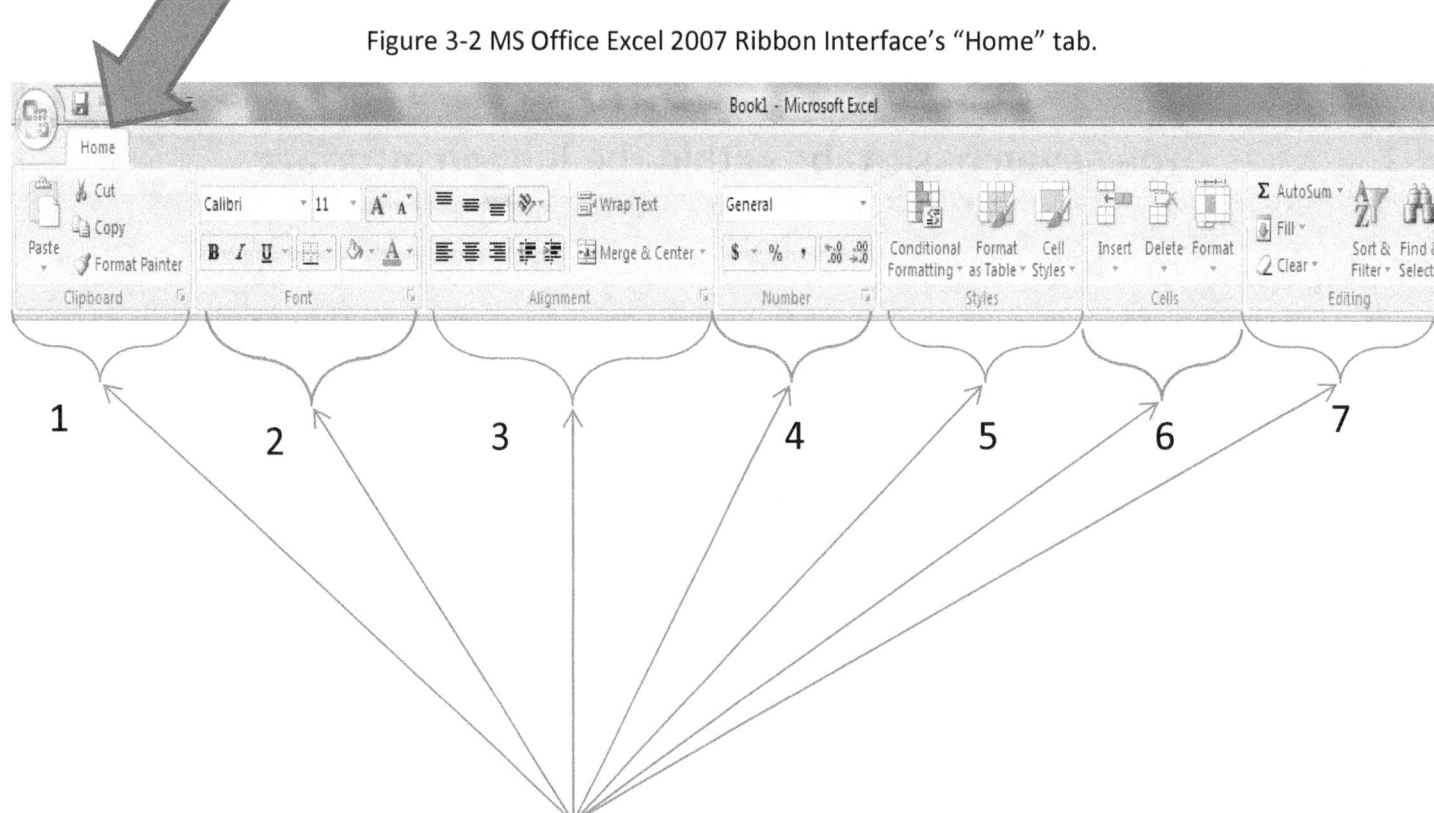

Figure 3-2 MS Office Excel 2007 Ribbon Interface's "Home" tab.

The Home tab is divided into seven easily identifiable groups:

1. Clipboard – The space where you temporarily hold data to be copied, paste or cut from cells in your spreadsheet.

2. Font – Size, bold, underline or color characters in your spreadsheet.

3. Alignment – Orient characters in the cells of your spreadsheet.

4. Number – Format numbers in spreadsheet to show as Currency or Percent or to contain commas.

5. Styles - Changes the looks of a cell or table based on the content of the cell or table

6. Cells – Insert or delete rows or columns in a Spreadsheet. Size or hide cells in a spreadsheet. Also add or duplicate worksheets in a spreadsheet.

7. Editing - Basic manipulation of data in spreadsheet (quickly filling cells with the same data; summing a column of data; finding a specified value in a spreadsheet; and sorting or filtering data in a spreadsheet).

The Insert tab

Ribbon Interface
Module 3

Figure 3-3 MS Office Excel 2007 Ribbon Interface's "Insert" tab.

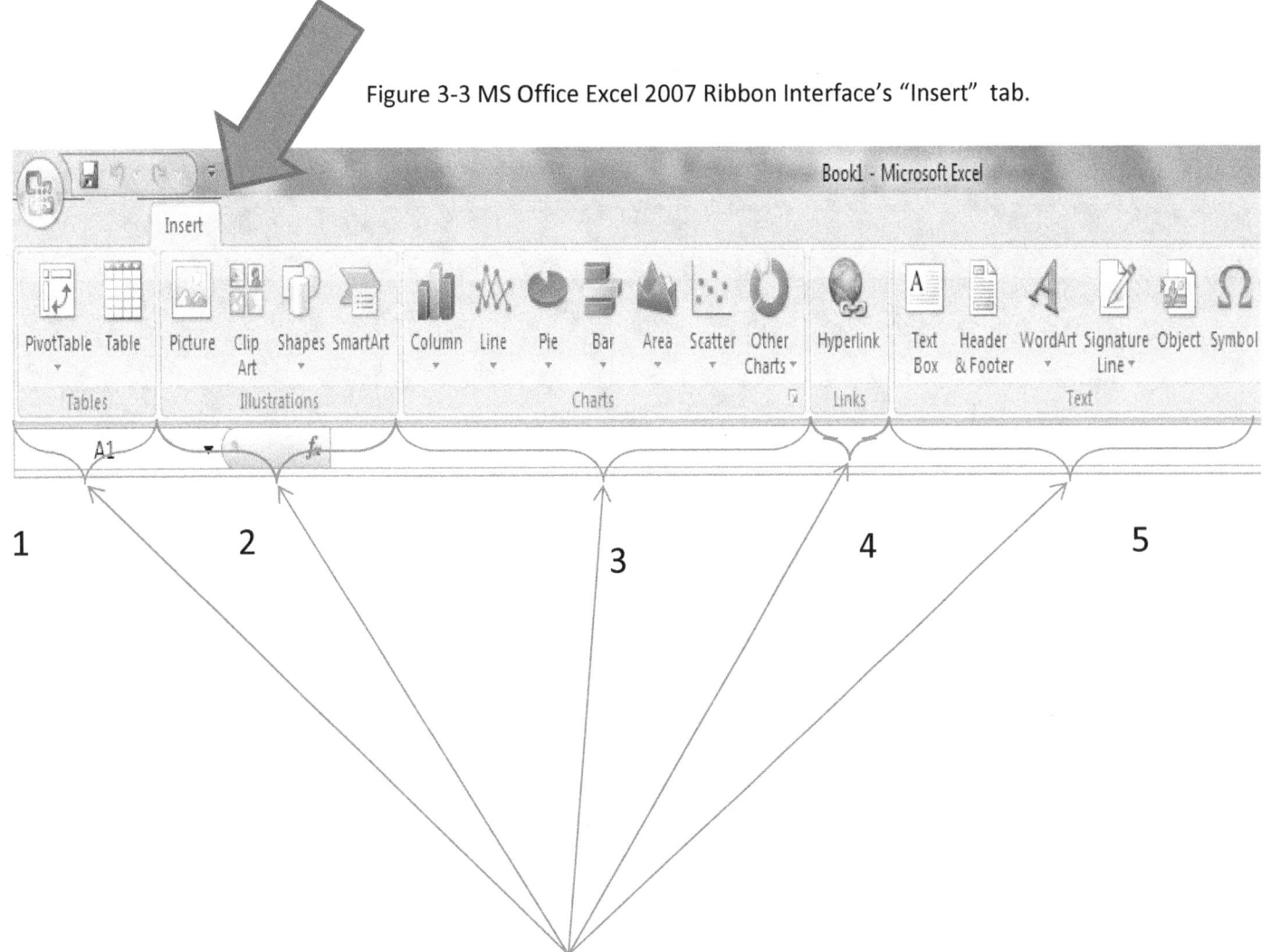

The Insert tab is divided into five easily identifiable groups:

1. Tables – Create data tables that will allow user to easily organize information. Insertion of data tables and /or pivot tables occur here.
2. Illustrations – Pictures, Clip Art or Shapes such as arrows, circles , squares, etc. can be inserted into your spreadsheet by using this feature.
3. Charts – This feature gives you the ability to graph your data so it can be easily analyzed. There are many grapJ types to choose from.
4. Links –Gives you the ability to add links to other worksheets or external data.
5. Text - Gives you the ability to add header and footers to spreadsheet; add text boxes to further explain a point in data; add unique symbols to your data or add WordArt text to emphasize a point in your data.

The Page Layout tab

Ribbon Interface
Module 3

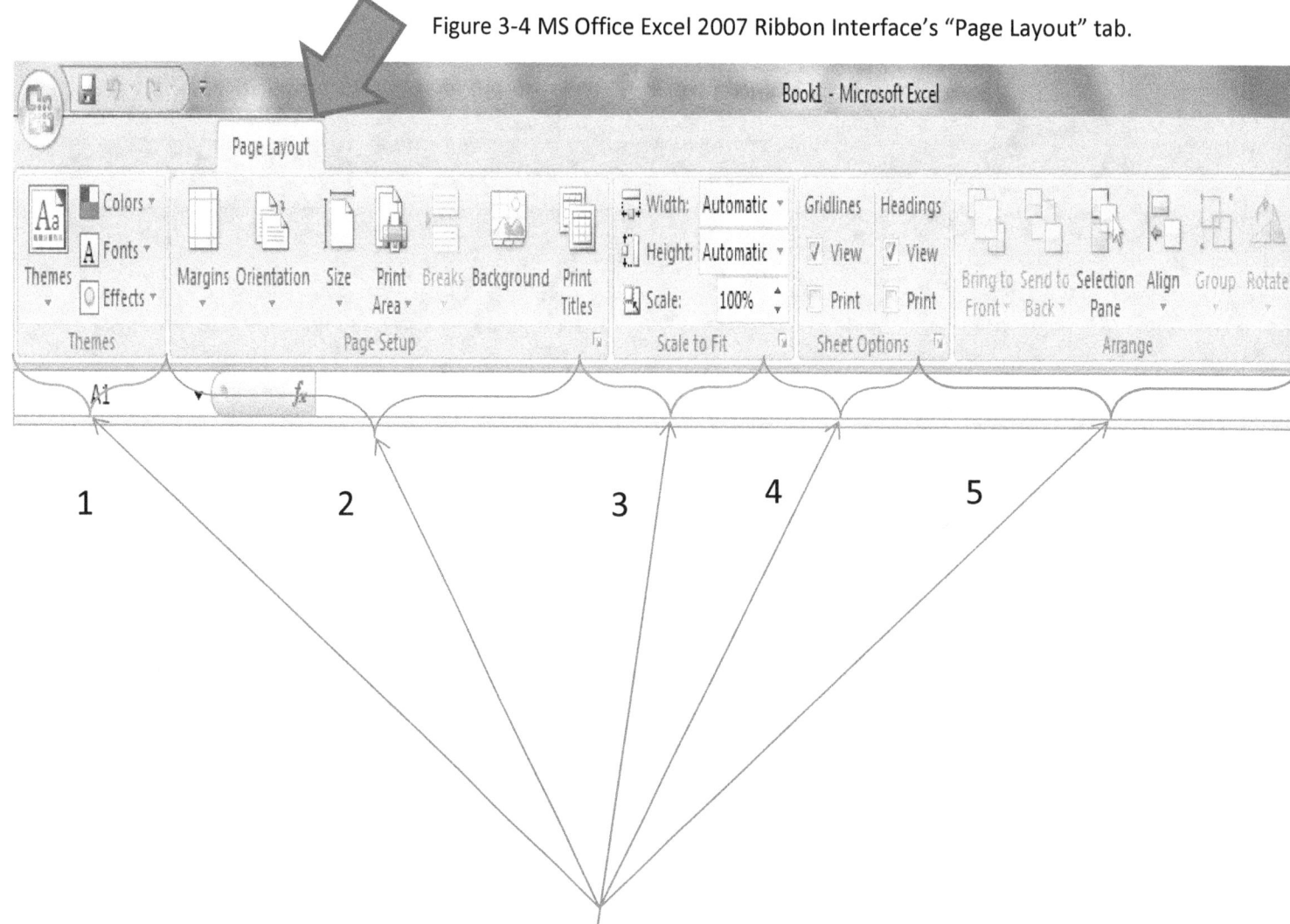

Figure 3-4 MS Office Excel 2007 Ribbon Interface's "Page Layout" tab.

The Page Layout tab is divided into five easily identifiable groups:

1. Themes – Change overall design of entire spreadsheet including colors, fonts and effect.

2. Page Setup – Change the page margins for the spreadsheet. Adjust Orientation (portrait and landscape). Select page size (8.5 x 11 , 8.5 x 14, 7.25 x 10.5, etc.). Ability to print some or all of the data contain within your spreadsheet. Ensure the same title is printed on top of your data when you have data that spans consecutive pages.

3. Scale to Fit – This feature gives you the ability to scale your data to fit on the number of pages your desire.

4. Sheet Options – Allows you to hide spreadsheet row headers and gridlines on the computer screen and on the printed document.

5. Arrange - Gives you ability to add clip art an pictures to your spreadsheet and to align , group , arrange or rotate the added art or picture.

The Formulas tab

Ribbon Interface
Module 3

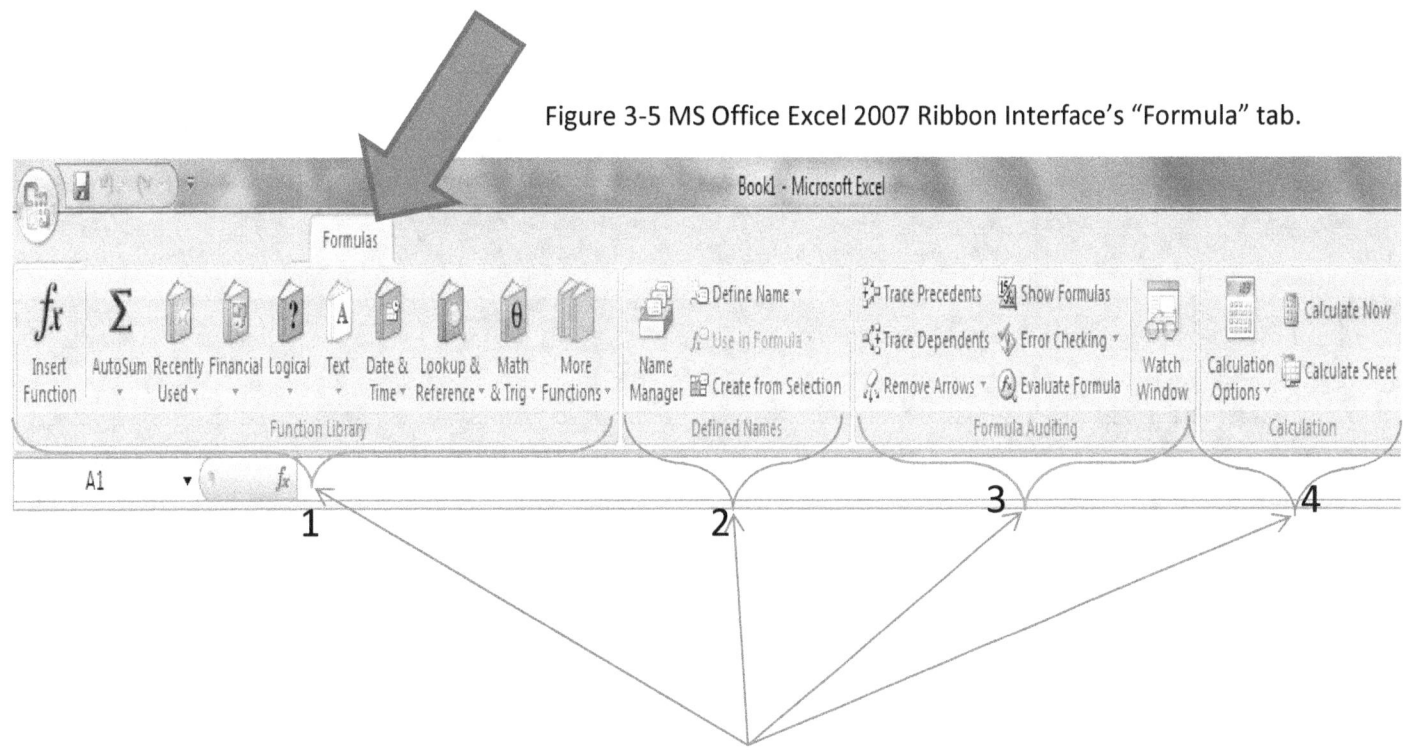

Figure 3-5 MS Office Excel 2007 Ribbon Interface's "Formula" tab.

he Formulas tab is divided into four easily identifiable groups:

.**Function Library** – Empowers you to add intelligence to your data. It gives you the bility to use different functions to help add intelligence to their data. Microsoft has ollected the most common functions used throughout academia and industry. ormulas are conveniently group by functions such as financial, logical , math & trig, tatistical and many more.

.**Defined Names** – Allows user to give a cell a defined name that can be easily used o refer to that cell when using formulas. This eliminates the need to remember row nd column numbers when managing your data.

.**Formula Auditing** – Gives you the ability to audit or check your formulas so you can ake sure they are doing what you intended for them to do.

.**Calculation** –Allows you to control when formulas calculate. By default, as soon as ou update a value that is tied to a formula excel will calculate and display the results nmediately in your spreadsheet. This is usually fine but sometimes you may want to ontrol when the calculation occurs so you can monitor the results. This is handled by etting the calculations feature in excel to Automatic or Manual.

The Data tab

Ribbon Interface
Module 3

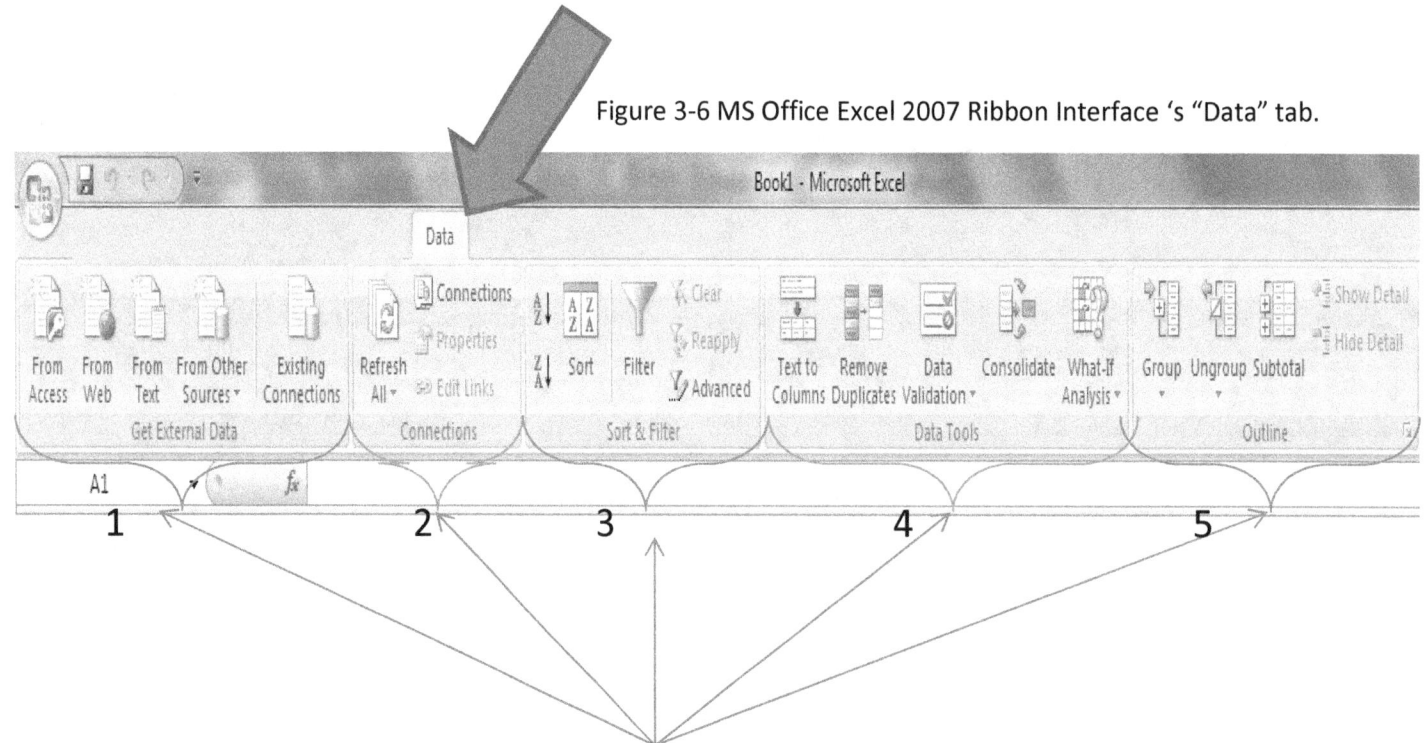

Figure 3-6 MS Office Excel 2007 Ribbon Interface 's "Data" tab.

The Data tab is divided into five easily identifiable groups:

1. Get External Data – Allows you to import data from tables in other data sources like an Access database or the internet, or a text document.

2. Connections – This feature when chosen alerts you of what external connections/data are linked to your spreadsheet. Also allows you to refresh your spreadsheet with data from your external data source.

3. Sort & Filter – This feature gives you the ability to sort or filter data in your spreadsheet.

4. Data Tools – Allows you to remove duplicate data, create validation conditions that must be met before data can be entered into a cell and provide you the ability to define ranges of cells from multiple worksheets to be summarized (averaged, summed, etc) showing results in one consolidation worksheet. Also allows you to test different data values in your spreadsheet formulas to see what would be the results.

5. Outline - Provides you the ability to group like data so it can be manage as a group. Also allows you to add subtotals to grouped data.

The Review tab

Ribbon Interface
Module 3

Figure 3-7 MS Office Excel 2007 Ribbon Interface 's "Review" tab.

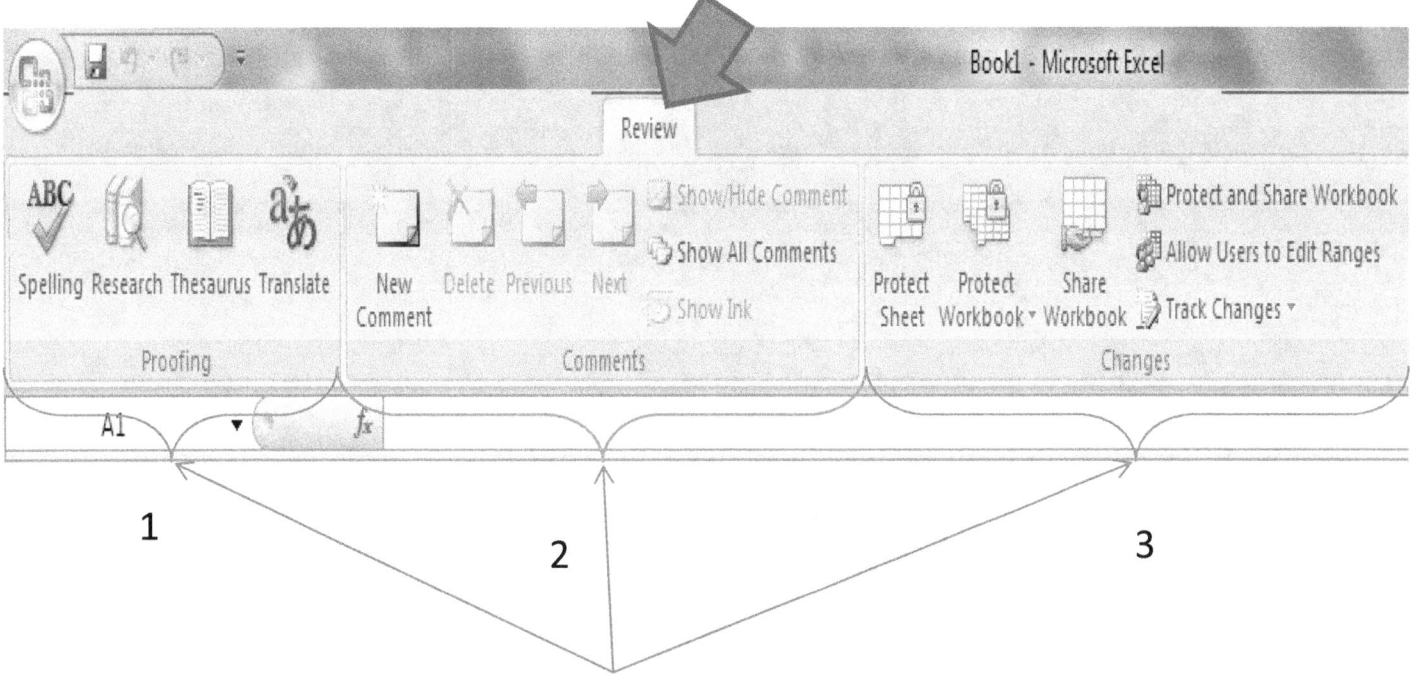

The Review tab is divided into three easily identifiable groups:
1.Proofing – Allows you to check the spelling in your spreadsheet. Also allows you to look up definitions, find similar words or translate words.
2.Comments – This feature will provides you the ability to add comments to your spreadsheet to further explain your data elements.
3.Changes – This feature gives you the ability to lock/protect cells in your spreadsheet from being edited. Also, if you add your spreadsheet to a network you can allow others to edit/update your shared spreadsheet/workbook.

The View tab

Ribbon Interface
Module 3

Figure 3-8 MS Office Excel 2007 Ribbon Interface's "View" tab.

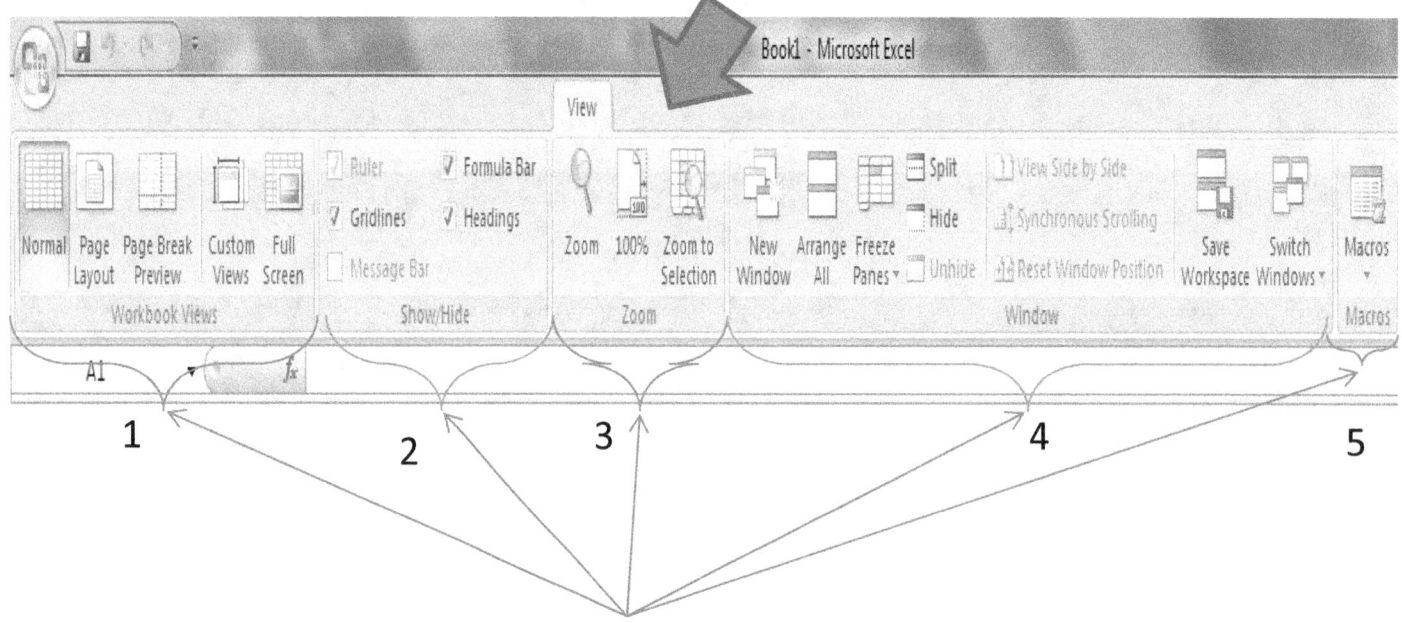

The View tab is divided into five easily identifiable groups:
1.Workbook Views – Provides you the capability to view how your spreadsheet data will be displayed on the printed page. Gives you the ability to adjust the page layout of the printed spreadsheet.
2.Show/Hide – This feature will allow you to hide or display spreadsheet gridlines. Also hide or show headings, ruler or formula bar.
3.Zoom – Provides you the ability to zoom in on a specific area of your spreadsheet.
4.Window – Allows you to open existing spreadsheet in a new window. You can also arrange all open spreadsheet on your screen so you can see and select which one you are interested in addressing. Allows you to freeze a row or column so that the frozen point is the new temporary starting point of where your scroll starts. Allow you to split your spreadsheet into sections on your screen to make it easier to navigate complex spreadsheets. Allows you to hide currently displayed spreadsheet from view. Finally the Window group will allow you to view multiple worksheets side by side . Especially useful when comparing an updated worksheet to an original.
5.Macros – The Macro feature allows you to create sophisticated formulas or logic to calculate or analyze your data.

What have you learned so far?

Figure 3-9 MS Office Excel 2007 Ribbon Interface tabs.

1) The Ribbon Interface **Home** tab, and the functions, within, its 7 groups.
2) The Ribbon Interface **Insert** tab, and the functions, within, its 5 groups.
3) The Ribbon Interface **Page Layout** tab, and the functions, within, its 5 groups.
4) The Ribbon Interface **Formulas** tab, and the functions, within, its 4 groups.
5) The Ribbon Interface **Data** tab, and the functions, within, its 5 groups.
6) The Ribbon Interface **Review** tab, and the functions, within, its 3 groups.
7) The Ribbon Interface **View** tab, and the functions, within, its 5 groups.

CREATING A SPREADSHEET
COLUMNS AND ROW...COLUMNS AND ROWS

Creating a Spreadsheet
Module 4

In this module you will begin implementing some of the features you learned in the previous module:

- Office Button Icon

- *Ribbon Interface* – **Insert tab**

- *Ribbon Interface* – **Home tab**

- *Ribbon Interface* – **Formulas tab**

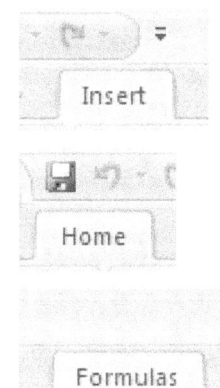

Figure 4 - 1 MS Office Excel 2007 Office Button and the Ribbon Interface's insert, home and formula tabs.

Data in spreadsheets are organized in Rows and Columns.

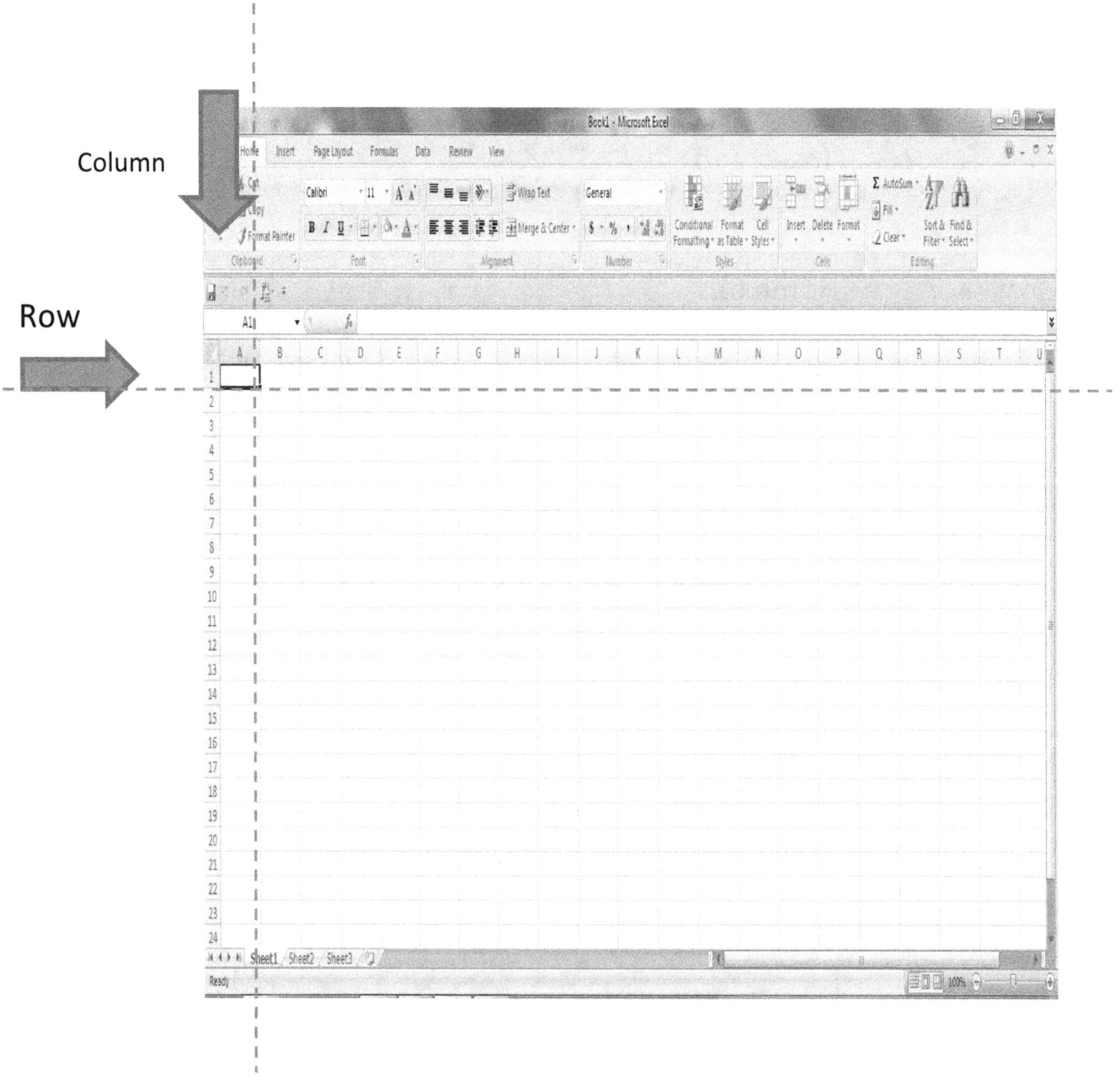

Figure 4-2 MS Office Excel 2007 worksheet.

An Excel spreadsheet will allow you to track and manage data. Listed below, are examples of data to be tracked or managed.

- Budget

- Employees

- Inventory

- Locations

- Salaries

- Events

Creating your first spreadsheet.

Creating a basic spreadsheet:

Scenario 1: A department within ACME company has 3 employees. The manager wants a method of tracking and managing his employees and their years of service.

Although you work in another department, the ACME manager heard that you just completed Excel training. So he requested that you help him develop this spreadsheet.

Access the "First Basic Spreadsheet Example_final version_module4.xlsx" from the CD that came with this manual to see hands-on examples Scenario 1, 2A, 2B, 2C, 2D, and 2E.

Creating a Spreadsheet
Module 4

Getting started creating a spreadsheet.

1) **Open** Excel. **Select**, the "Office Button Icon". **Select**, "New", from the pull down menu. **Select**, "Create" button, located on the bottom right of the screen.

Creating headers or field names for your first spreadsheet.

2) Type, the following information in the first three cells in Row 1.

Type, "Last Name", in Row 1, column A.
Type, "First Name", in Row 1, column B.
Type, " Years of Service", in Row 1, column C.
　　Note: These entries are the headers or field names which describe the type of data that will be populated in each column.

Creating Data for your first spreadsheet.

3) Type, in the first three cells, in Row 2, the following information:

　　Type, "Patton", in Row 2, column A.
　　Type, "George", in Row 2, column B.
　　Type, "32", in Row 2, column C.

4) Type the following information, in the first three cells, in Row 3.

　　Type, "Eisenhower", in Row 3, column A.
　　Type, "Dwight", in Row 3, column B.
　　Type, "5", in Row 3, column C.

5) Type, the following information, in the first three cells, in Row 4.

　　Type, "Principal", in Row 4, column A.
　　Type, "Victoria", in Row 4, column B.
　　Type, "12", in Row 4, column C.

Note: Items 3 thru 5 are your data.

Creating a Spreadsheet
Module 4

First basic spreadsheet example.

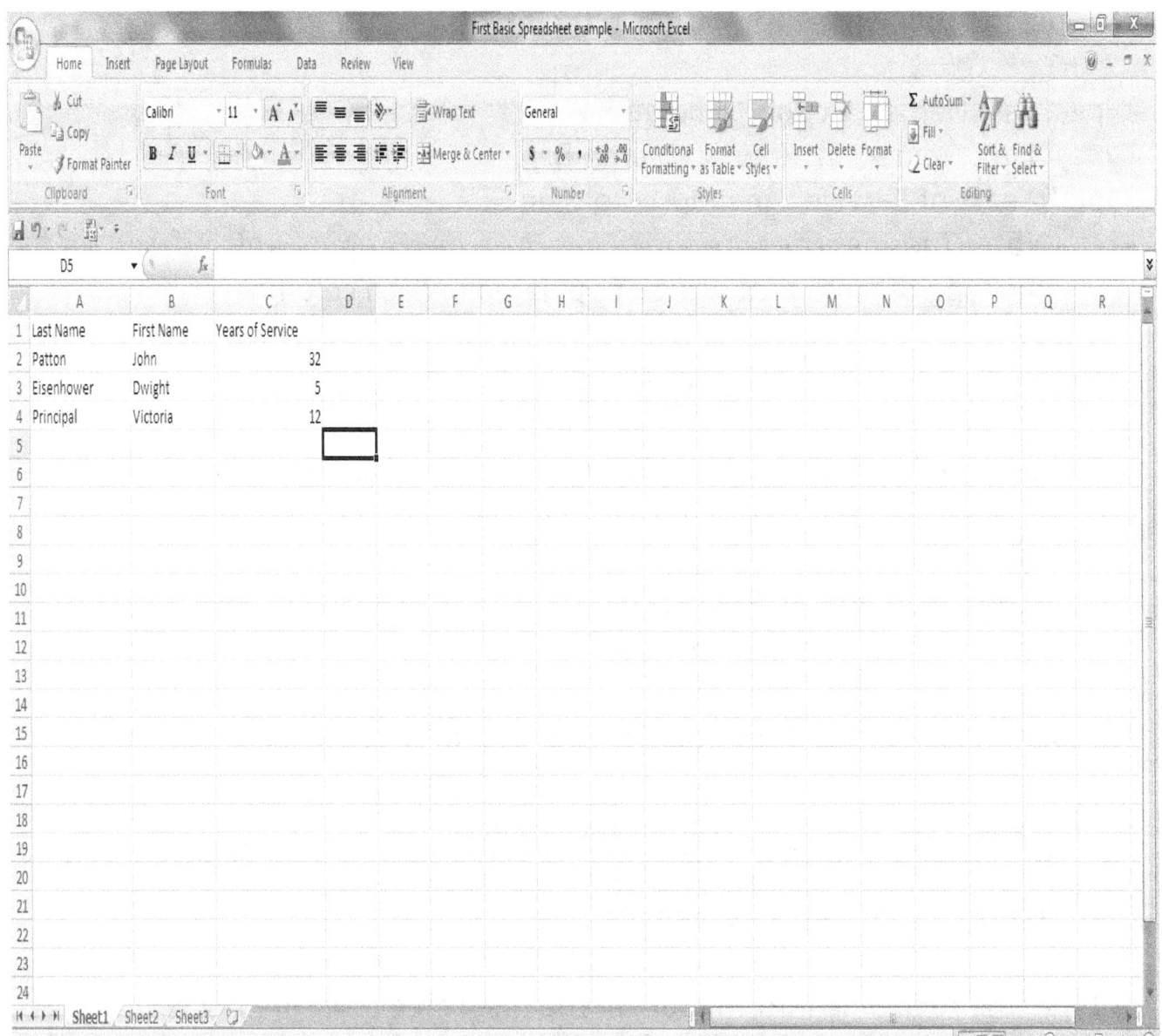

Figure 4-3 MS Office Excel 2007 First Basic spreadsheet example..

Now, as shown on the previous page, you have created a very basic spreadsheet. This spreadsheet allows you to track ACME's 3 employees and their years of service.

Once, this information was presented to ACME's management team, it was decided there were other uses for the data. They concluded the spreadsheet could be used to help better manage their entire workforce.

Scenario 2:

Management wants to now know how many junior and senior employees are in the ACME department. They want to know which employees are eligible to mentor newer employees, based on their years of service (> 10 years). They also want to know when an employee is about to reach a milestone or anniversary. And they want to know, which employees are eligible for more responsibility based on their years of service. Finally, they need to know which employees are about to retire.

Statistical information regarding employees was also requested. Management will use it during resource discussion with the Human Resource office. Information such as, "Average" and "Median" years of service.

Data management through the use of Formulas.

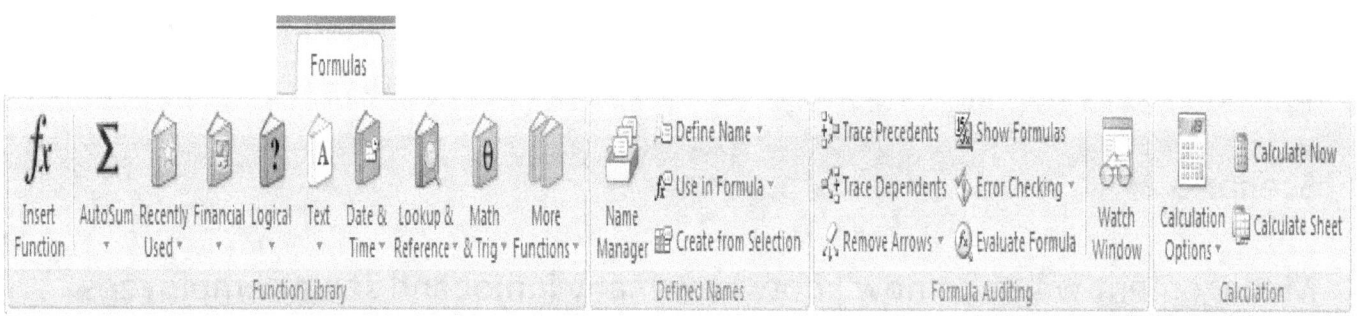

Figure 4-4 MS Office Excel 2007 Ribbon Interface 's "Formula" tab.

Lets review the requirements given to you by ACME's management:

A) Need **Total** years of service for all employees combined.
B) Need **Average** years of service for all employees combined.
C) Need **Median** years of service for all employees combined.
D) Need to be able to quickly discern, via text description, the **seniority levels** (junior, senior) of the employees. Seniors are considered **> 10 years**.
E) Finally, need to know an employee's next **milestone (5, 10, 20, 30, 40, 50 years)**.

Using the Sum function located on Home tab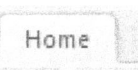

Scenario 2-A:

We will first satisfy Requirement A using your basic spreadsheet.
Requirement (A) - **"Total** years of service for all employees combined".

Within your first basic spreadsheet,
- place your cursor on cell C5 (this is row 5 column C).
- Press your left mouse button, once, to highlight this cell.

Now, go to the Ribbon Interface.
- Select the Home tab.
- Go to the "Editing Group" on the Home tab.
- Select AutoSum (cells C2 thru C4 will be highlighted).
- Choose the <Enter> key on your Keyboard.

Next,
- place your cursor on cell B5.
- Press, your left mouse button once to highlight this cell .
- Type, "Total Combined Employee Years".

Congratulations, requirement (A) is Complete. See figure 4-5.

Requirement (A) – "Total years of service for all employees combined".

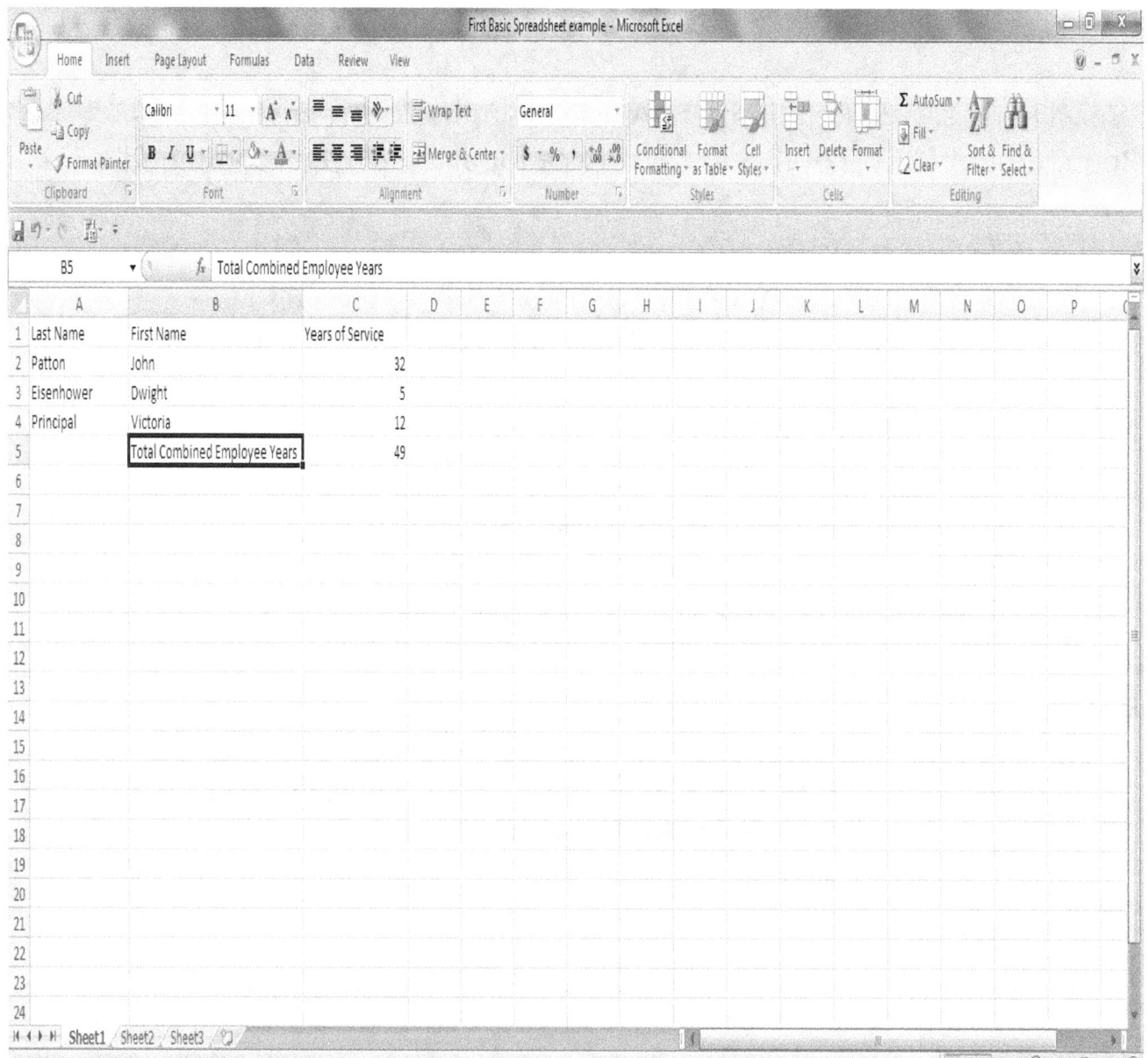

Figure 4-5 MS Office Excel 2007 First Basic spreadsheet example with Sum formula function included.

Creating a Spreadsheet
Module 4

Using the **Average** function found on Formulas tab

Formulas

Scenario 2-B:

Next, within your basic spreadsheet you will satisfy requirement B. Requirement (B) - Need **Average** years of service for all employees combined.

Within your First basic spreadsheet,
- place your cursor on cell C6 (this is row 6 column C).
- Press, your left mouse button once to highlight this cell.

Now, go to the Ribbon Interface,
- Select the Formulas tab.
- Go to the "Function Library" group, on the Formulas tab.
- Select "More Functions", from the Function Library group.
- Select "Statistical", from the drop down menu.
- Select "Average", from the choices provided.
- On the "Function Arguments" popup menu select cell "Number 1", and type "C2:C4".
- Select, the <OK> button on the bottom right side of the "Function Arguments" popup menu.

Next,
- place your cursor on cell B6.
- Press, your left mouse button once, to highlight this cell.
- Type, "Employees Average Years of Service".

Congratulations, requirement (B) is complete. See Figure 4-6.

Requirement (B) – "Average years of service for all employees combined".

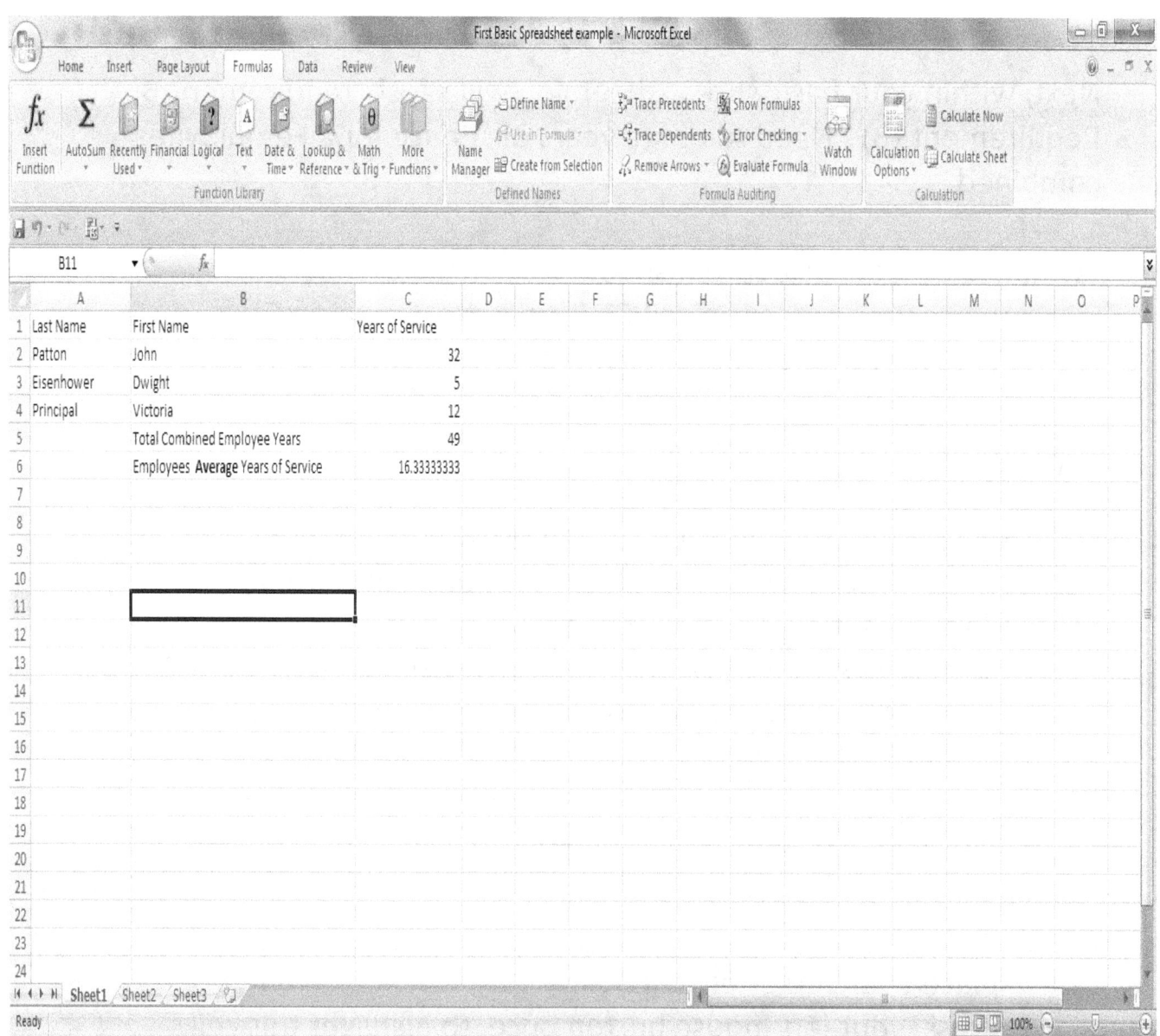

Figure 4-6 MS Office Excel 2007 First Basic spreadsheet example with Sum and Average formula functions included.

Using the Median function located on the Formulas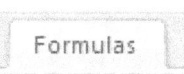

Scenario 2-C:

Next, using your basic spreadsheet you will satisfy requirement (C):
Requirement (C)– "Need **Median** years of service for all employees combined".

Within your First Basic Spreadsheet,

- place your cursor, on cell C7 (this is row 7 column C).
- Press, your left mouse button, once, to highlight this cell.

Now go to the Ribbon Interface,

- Select the Formulas tab.
- Go to the "Function Library" group, on the Formulas tab.
- Select "More Functions" from the Function Library group.
- Select "Statistical" from the drop down menu.
- Select "Median" from the choice provided.
- On the "Function Arguments" popup menu select cell "Number 1", then select the "Collapse Dialog icon", in the right corner .

Using the Median function found on Formulas tab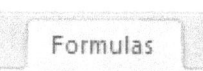

Next,
- place your cursor on cell C2   (this is row 2 column C) .
- Press, and hold down your left mouse button while you scroll from C2 to C4.
- Release the left mouse button (C2 through C4 should be highlighted with blinking dashed lines).

Now,
- Select the <Enter> key on your keyboard (the "Function Arguments" popup menu, will expand with your values, "C2:C4", showing in the "Number 1" cell).
- Select the "OK" button located on the bottom right side of the "Function Arguments" popup menu.

Next,
- place your cursor on cell B7.
- Press your left mouse button once to highlight this cell.
- Type, "Employees Median Years of Service".

Congratulations, requirement (C) is complete. See figure 4-7

Requirement (C) "Median years of service for all employees combined".

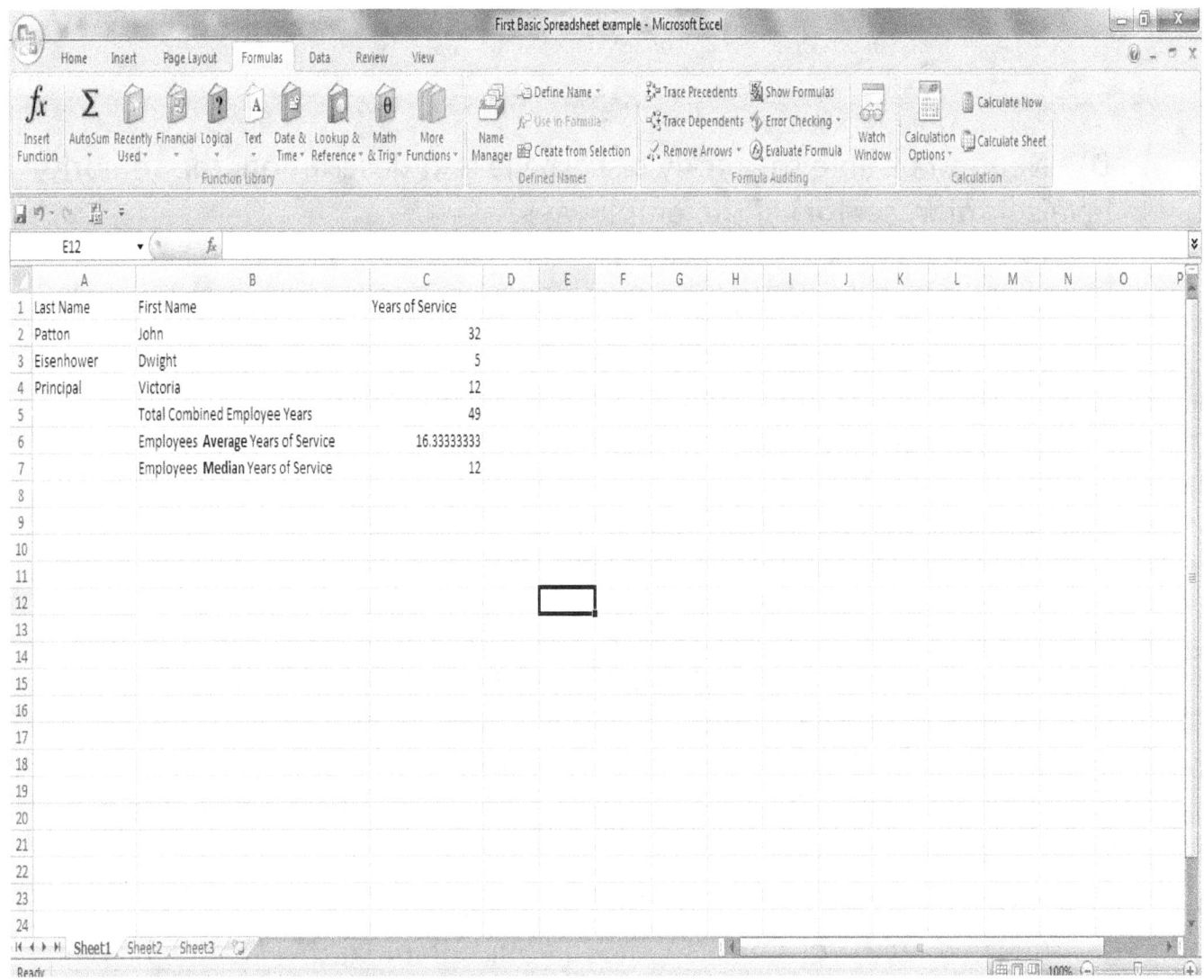

Figure 4-7 MS Office Excel 2007 First Basic spreadsheet example with Sum, Average and Median formula functions included.

Using the logical IF function located on the Formulas tab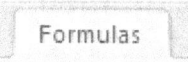

Scenario 2-D:

D) - Need to be able to quickly discern via text description, the seniority levels **(junior, senior)** of the employees.

Within your First Basic Spreadsheet,

- place your cursor on cell D2 (this is row 2 column D).
- Press your left mouse button once, to highlight this cell.

Now go to the Ribbon Interface,

- Select the "Formulas" tab.
- Go to the "Function Library" group on the "Formulas" tab.
- Select "Logical" from the "Function Library" group.
- Select "IF" from the choice provided.
- On the "Function Arguments" popup menu select cell, "Logical Test" .
- In the "Logical _Test" cell, type, "C2 > 10".
- Now, with your mouse, move your cursor to the "Value_if_True" cell and click once.
- Next, type into the "Value_if_True" cell, "senior".
- Next, with your mouse, move your cursor to the "Value_if_False" cell and click once.
- Next, type into the "Value_if_False" cell, "junior".
- Select the <OK> button on the right bottom side of the "Function Arguments" popup menu.

Using the logical IF function located on the Formulas tab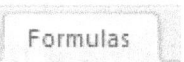

- Place you cursor on cell D2 and click the right mouse button.

A popup menu will appear.
- Select "copy".

Next,
- place your cursor on cell D3.
- Press, the left mouse button once and drag the cursor to D4 (both cells D3 and D4 will be highlighted).

Next,
- click the right mouse button once more.

A popup menu will appear.
- Select "paste".

Finally,
- place your cursor on cell D1.
- Press your left mouse button once to highlight this cell, then type "Seniority".

The "IF" logic you just created will accomplish the following:
If the employee's years of service is greater than 10, then they are considered a "Senior". If it is less than or equal to 10 years, they are considered a "Junior".

Congratulations, requirement (D) is complete. See Figure 4-8.

Requirement (D) – "The seniority levels (junior, senior) of the employees".

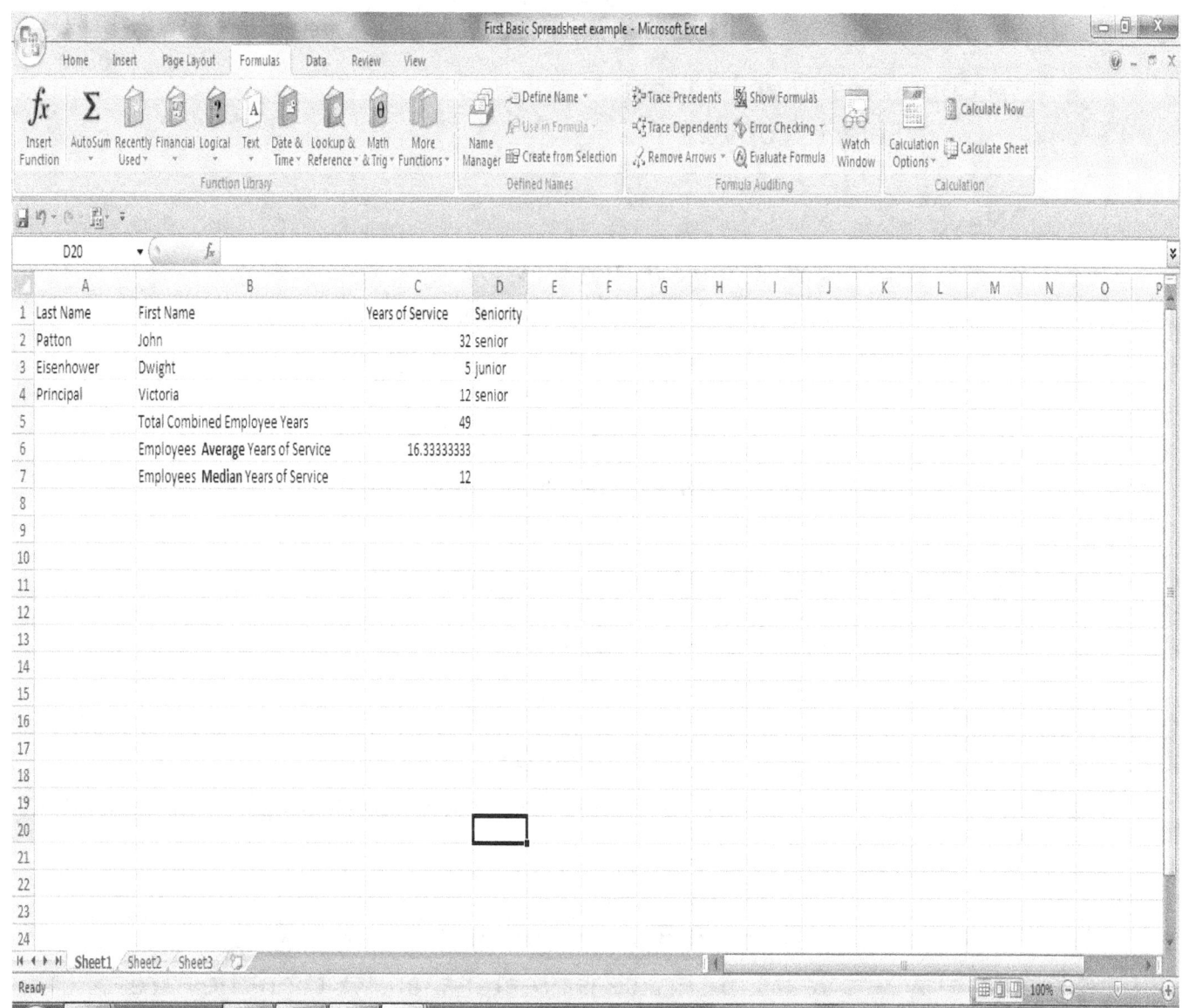

Figure 4-8 MS Office Excel 2007 First Basic spreadsheet example with Sum, Average, Median and custom Seniority formula functions added.

Using the logical IF function located on the Formulas tab

Scenario 2-E:

E) What is an employee's next **milestone (5, 10, 20, 30, 40 or 50 years)**.

Within your first basic spreadsheet,
- place your cursor on cell E2 (this is row 2 column E).
- Press, your left mouse button once to highlight this cell.
- Next, type the following into cell E2:

=IF(50/C2<1.28,"50 year pin",IF(50/C2<1.72,"40 year pin", IF(50/C2<2.63,"30 year pin",IF(50/C2<5.6,"20 year pin",IF(50/C2<12.5,"10 year pin","5 year pin")))))

Note: Please do not omit any parenthesis or commas or quotes. If you do, the above formula, will not work.

Now,
- place you cursor on cell E2 and click the right mouse button.
- A popup menu will appear. Select, "copy".

Next,
- place your cursor on cell E3, press the left mouse button once and drag the cursor to E4 (both cells E3 and E4 will be highlighted).

Finally,
- Click, the right mouse button once more (a popup menu will appear).
- Select "paste".
- Place your cursor on cell E1.
- Press your left mouse button once to highlight this cell and type "Next Milestone".

Congratulations, requirement (E) is Complete. See Figure 4-9.

Requirement (E) - "Employees next milestones".

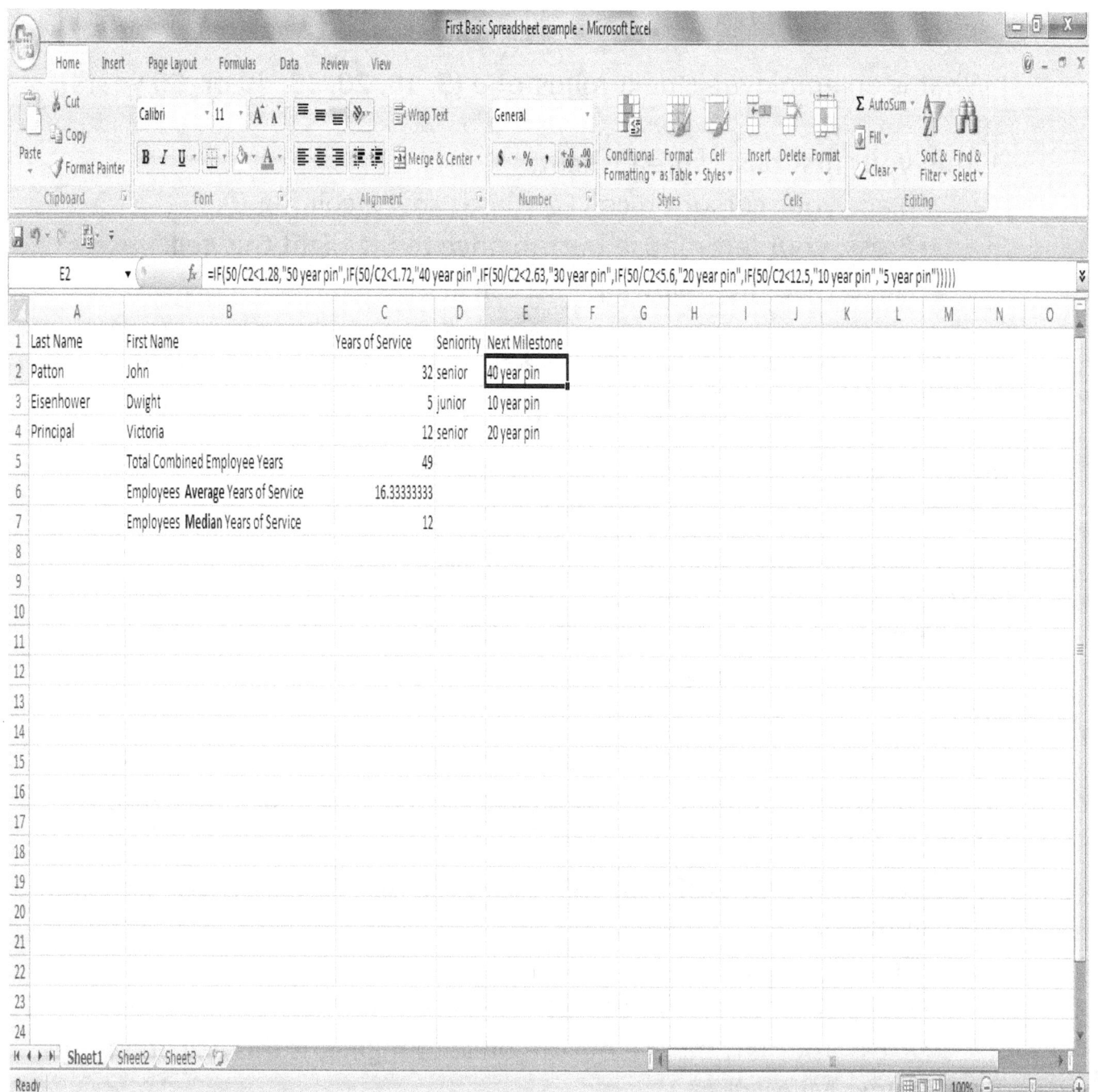

Figure 4-9 MS Office Excel 2007 First Basic spreadsheet example with Sum, Average, Median and custom Seniority and Milestone formulas added.

Creating a Spreadsheet
Module 4

What have you learned so far?

1) How to create spreadsheet.
2) How to **Sum,** a column of data, using the Sum Σ function located on the Home tab.
3) How to **Average,** a column of data, using the Average function located on the Formulas tab.
4) How to get the **Median,** of a column of data, using the Median function located on the Formulas tab.
5) How to use the **IF** Logical function located on the Formulas tab, to help the user to interpret a row of data.
6) How to write a logical **IF** statement without the assistance of the "Function Arguments" menu, to help the user interpret row data.

CREATING A TABLE ONE RECORD AT A TIME

Now, that you have learned how to create a spreadsheet, you are ready to start creating **data tables** in Excel.

A table, in Excel gives the user the ability to relate data in a record format. Each row of data, becomes a record, while each column's element becomes a field in the record.

A row (record) might describe inventory item, request ticket, invoice or customer, to name a few. The column (field) for a record can contain invoice number, request number, customer name, etc.

Scenario #3:

The ACME Dept. Manager, wants to create a data table out of your basic spreadsheet. He also wants a few more columns (fields) added, so he can better manage his organization.

The additional columns (fields) are as follows:

- **Start Date**
- **Salary**
- **Health Benefits**
- **Job title**
- **401K**
- **Pension Plan**
- **Employee ID**

Access the "Converting First Basic Spreadsheet to a Data Table_module5.xlsx" from the CD that came with this manual to see hands-on examples Scenario 3, 3A, 3B, and 3C.

Creating a Data Table
Module 5

The ACME Dept. manager requested that the following information (Figure 5-1) be added to the columns requested.

	John	Dwight	Victoria
Start Date	1-May-80	5-Jan-07	1-Jun-90
Salary	50000	15000	35000
Health Benefits	Y	N	Y
Job Title	Supply Mgr	Supply Tech	Inventory Mgr
401K	Y	Y	Y
Pension Plan	Y	N	Y
Employid	00001	00002	00003

Figure 5-1 ACME Department mangers additional data request.

Creating a Data Table
Module 5

Adding Columns to the first basic spreadsheet.

Scenario 3 (continued):

1) Type the following information into the first three cells in Row 1.
   Type "Start Date", in Row 1, column F.
   Type "Salary", in Row 1, column G.
   Type "Health Benefits", in Row 1, column H.
   Type "Job Title", in Row 1, column I.
   Type "401K", in Row 1, column J.
   Type "Pension Plan", in Row 1, column K.
   Type "Employid", in Row 1, column L.

   Note: The entries above, are your column headers (field names), which describes, the type of data that will be populated in each column.

2) Type the following information, in Column F, Rows 2, 3, and 4.
   Type, "1-May-80", in Row 2, column F.
   Type, "5-Jan-07", in Row 3, column F.
   Type, "1-Jun-90", in Row 4, column F.

3) Type the following information, in Column G, Rows 2, 3, and 4.
   Type, "50000", in Row 2, column G.
   Type, "15000", in Row 3, column G.
   Type, "35000", in Row 4, column G.

   Note: The entries above, in items 2 and 3, are your data elements.

4) Type the following information, in Column H, Rows 2, 3, and 4.
   Type "Y", in Row 2, column H.
   Type "N", in Row 3, column H.
   Type "Y", in Row 4, column H.

5) Type the following information, in Column I, Rows 2, 3, and 4.
   Type "Supply Manager", in row 2, column I.
   Type "Supply Tech", in row 3, column I.
   Type "Inventory Manager", in row 4, column I.

6) Type in Column J, Rows 2, 3, and 4, the following information.
   Type "Y", in row 2, column J.
   Type "Y", in row 3, column J.
   Type "Y", in row 4, column J.

7) Type in Column K, Rows 2, 3, and 4, the following information.
   Type "Y", in row 2, column K.
   Type "N", in Row 3, column K.
   Type "Y", in row 4, column K.

8) Type the following information, in Column L, Rows 2, 3, and 4.
   Type "00003", in row 2, column L.
   Type "00016", in row 3, column L.
   Type "00010", in row 4, column L.

Please note the above entries are your data elements.

Creating a Data Table
Module 5

Your first basic spreadsheet (updated with the additional columns).

Scenario 3:

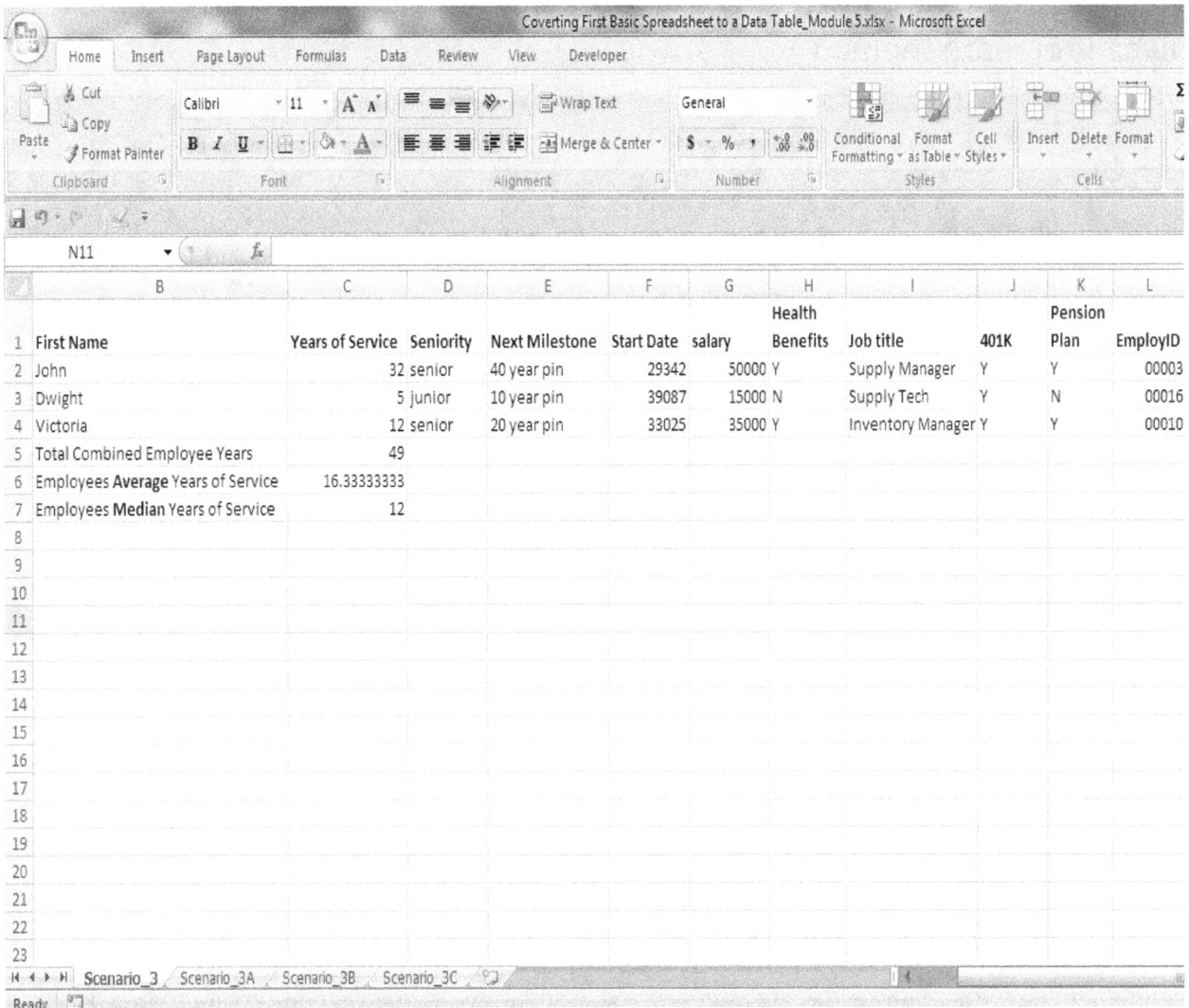

Figure 5-2 MS Excel 2007 Basic Spreadsheet example with additional columns added.

Creating a Data Table
Module 5

Preparing our basic spreadsheet's data so it can be converted to a data table.

Scenario 3-A:

The Total, Median and Average formulas you added to your original first basic spreadsheet, are not necessary for your data table. If you need them later, you can recreate them.

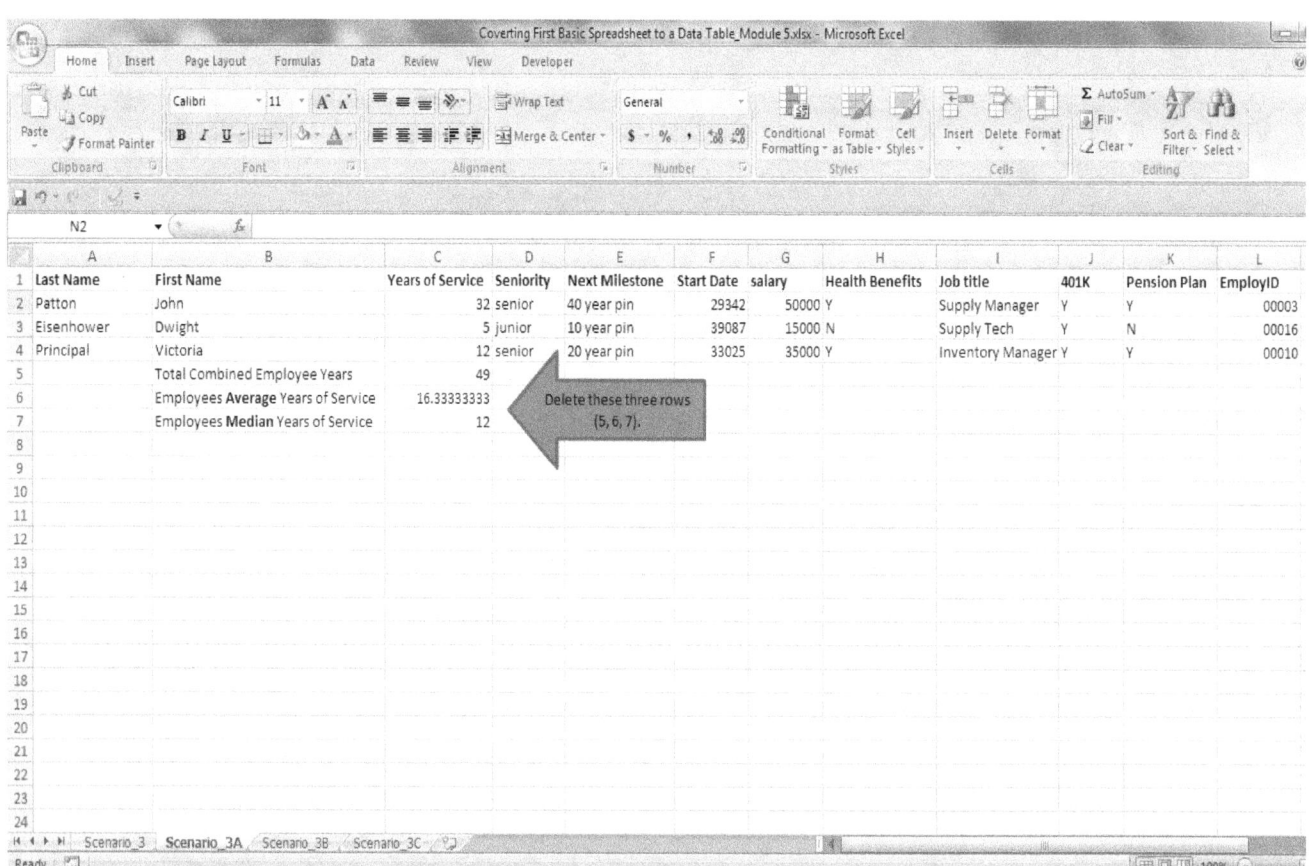

Figure 5-3 MS Excel 2007 Basic Spreadsheet example with information identified to be removed.

The revised basic spreadsheet with the requested additional columns.

Scenario 3-B

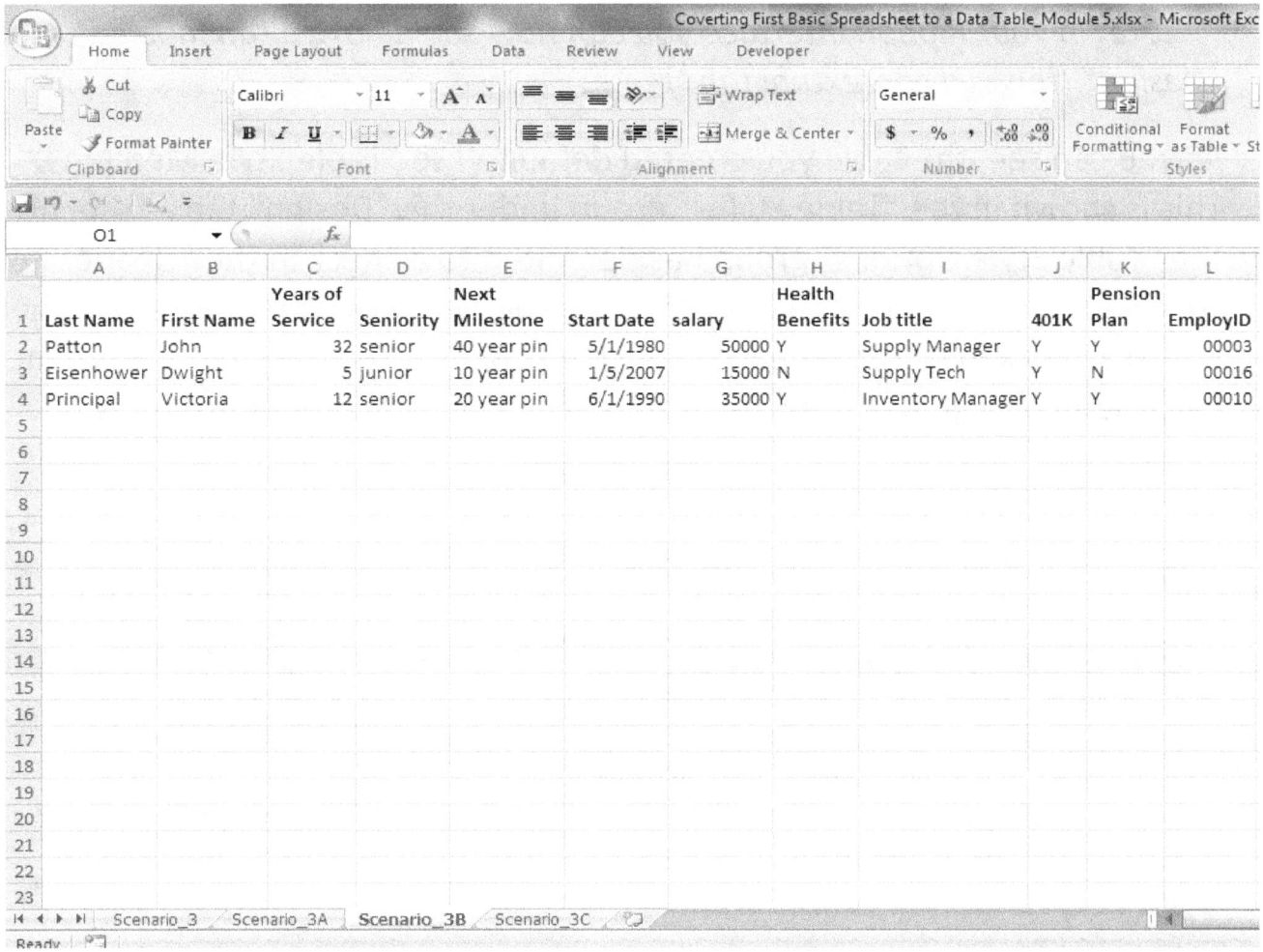

Figure 5-4 MS Excel 2007 Basic Spreadsheet example with added columns.

Creating a Data Table
Module 5

Scenario 3-C

1) Place cursor on row 1, Column A and left click once.
2) Next, select the "Insert" tab on the Ribbon Interface. As you can see, row A1 thru L1, are highlighted.
3) Next, select "Table" from the "Tables" group on the Ribbon Interface.
   Note: *In your Ribbon Interface you can now see an extra tab labeled "Design" (this is a contextual tab*).*

As you can see, the table you created defaulted to "Table Style Medium 9" . This is shown in the "Table Styles" group under the "Design" tab. Also, note the "Table Style Options" group has defaulted to a check in the "Header Row" checkbox . This allows for a header row to be displayed for your table. There is also a check in the "Banded Rows" checkbox. This will cause row content to be banded or highlighted by using different row colors for alternate rows.

Congratulations, you have created a Data Table within Excel.

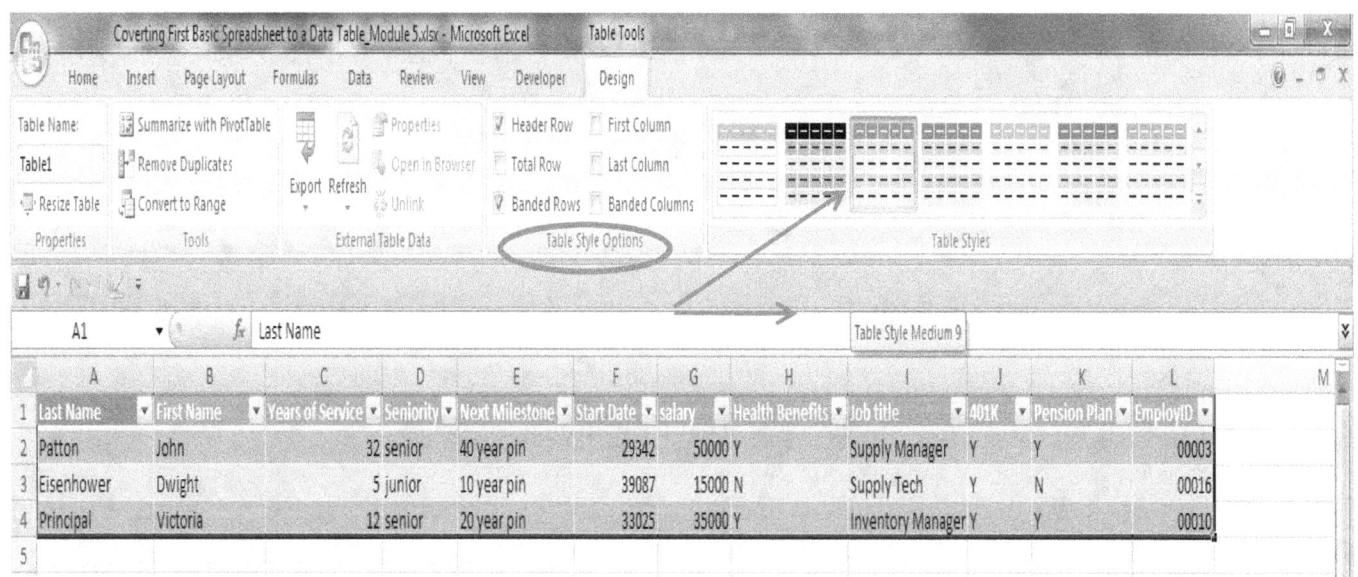

Figure 5-5 MS Excel 2007 Data Table.

*Contextual tabs appear in the Ribbon Interface only when an object is selected. For example, when you inserted the table object into your spreadsheet, the cursor came to rest on the active cell "A1" in your table object. This caused the "Design" tab to appear. Move your cursor outside of the table object to row "M1" and you'll notice the "Design" tab goes away.

Creating a Data Table
Module 5

Each row in our newly defined table represents a record. Now management has the ability to better manage the information (records) in this data table.

Notice there is a drop-down arrow ▼ button located, in each header (**fig. 5-6**). A drop-down arrow means that filtering is enabled, but not applied. When filtering is applied, only data specific to your filter is displayed in your data table.

When you hover with your mouse over the heading of a column with filtering enabled, but not applied, a screen tip displays the words, "(Showing All)". When a drop-down arrow button, has a funnel icon ▽ displayed in the header, it means that filtering has been applied.

Personal exercise: Practice filtering information in your data table.

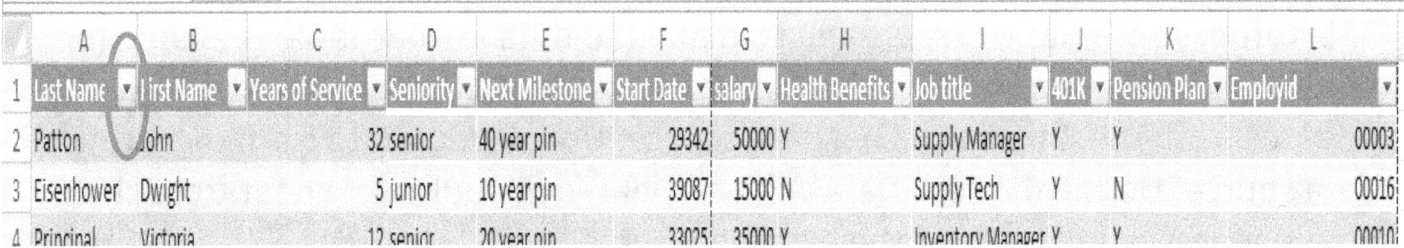

Figure 5-6 MS Excel 2007 Data Table with filter icons in header.

When the data table was created a "Design" tab appeared in the Ribbon Interface. This tab allows you to further define the capabilities and features for the data table.

Figure 5-7 MS Excel 2007 Ribbon Interface Design tab.

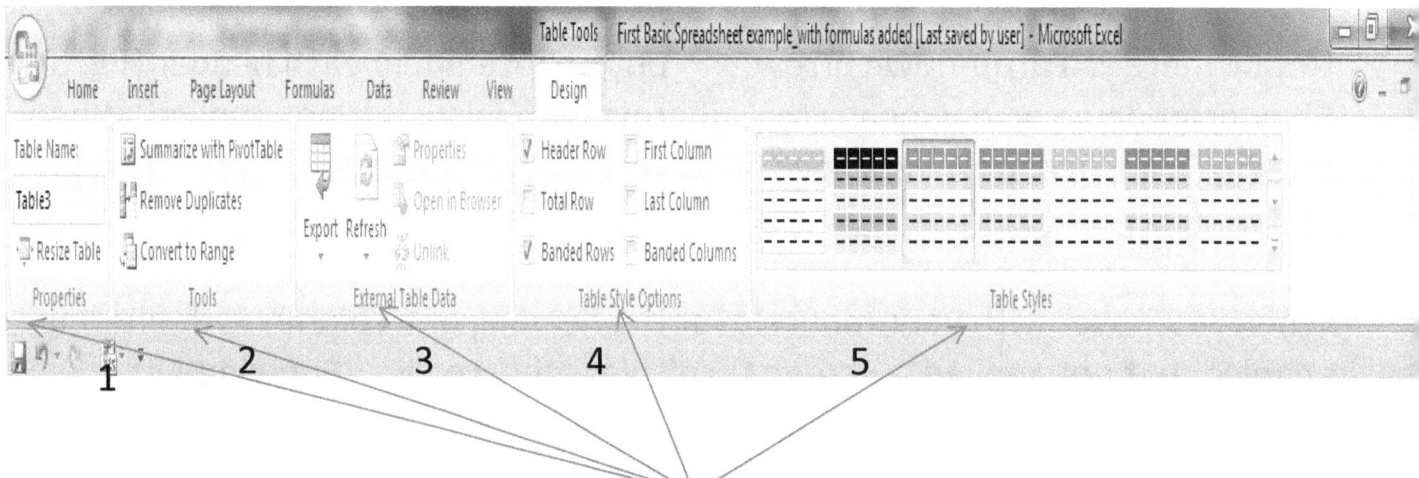

The Design tab is divided into five easily identifiable groups:
1. Properties Allows you to name your Table, so you can refer to it, in formulas. Also within this group, you can resize, the Table, by adding columns or rows.
2. Tools – Allows you to convert the table back to a spreadsheet range, remove duplicate rows, or create PivotTable (we will discuss this feature in the Pivot Table section of this booklet).
3. External Table Data– Allows you to make the data in your table available for editing by others via a website, using MS Sharepoint. Refresh your data with updates from the linked external data source. Unlink your data from the external data source. Define how the data will be updated in your worksheet from the data updates being made at the external source.
4. Table Style Options –Allows you to hide or show your column (field) headers; display or not display color bands on your table rows or columns; total a row of data; and make the first or last column a solid color fill.
5. Table Styles - Allows you to choose from a list of table colors that contain solid headers and banded rows.

What have you learned so far?

1) How to convert a spreadsheet range of data into a data table.
2) How to filter data once it is in a data table.
3) How to Style (color, rows and columns) a data table.
4) The groups and functions within the contextual "Design" tab.

Module 6

PIVOTTABLE DATA ANALYSIS

DEFINITION:

Pivot: person or thing on which something depends or turns; the central or crucial factor.

Take, as an example, that a person is handed an object that he or she has never seen before and is asked, "what is it?". The person will usually spin the object around, looking at it from all sides to get a clue about the nature of the object.

The same concept applies to a PivotTable report. It allows a user to place data in a PivotTable to enable the user to answer questions about the meaning of the data. The PivotTable will allow the user to view the data from various vantage points.

Many times when handed a data rich Excel spreadsheet or data table, it is not easy to understand what the data means. So what good is it to the person reviewing it if they can not gain any insight from it?

PivotTable reports allows a user to extract meaning from Excel data. No matter how simple or complex the data. PivotTables provide the means to extract facts, trends and patterns that are buried in data.

First, there are features of the PivotTable that you must understand before attempting to use it. In this module, we will discuss the following features.

PivotTable Features:

- Rows

- Columns

- Values

- Filters

Before you physically access the PivotTable and its features, we will discuss the concept behind using PivotTables.

What is the pivot point of your data?

When using a PivotTable report to better explain your Excel data you should consider the data's pivot point. To identify the pivot point, ask yourself, "what question am I attempting to answer?". You must know the question being asked because it is key to you picking the field(s) that will provide the correct answer.

The Excel data fields you select to answer a question are considered the pivot points. When using the PivotTable Feature within Excel these fields will be presented to you in a selection list. The names of the fields listed in the selection list are the header names of the Excel data you are examining. Data from the fields you select as pivot points will be displayed across the rows and columns of your PivotTable Report. When an answer to a question requires only one field (pivot point), you have the option to display the answer through the use of rows only. Questions whose answers require the use of multiple fields are best displayed across both rows and columns. In this manual we will show examples of both.

Sometimes, to better interpret the PivotTable Report, the results need to be summarized or grouped. The PivotTable function will provide various settings (i.e Total, Sum , Average, etc.) for you to choose from to summarize your answer. The smmary setting that you select will be displayed at the end of your PivotTable report's rows or at the bottom of the columns.

PivotTable Features

We will now discuss the features within the PivotTable that are to be used to generate answers to your questions. These features will be used in the exercises that will be presented later in this module.

PivotTable – Data Analysis
Module 6

To access the PivotTable features you will highlight your excel data then select the **Insert tab** from the Ribbon Interface (**figure 6-1**). Next, by selecting the **PivotTable Icon** from the **Tables** group, you will be given the option to create a PivotTable Report (**figure 6-2**). Select "Ok" from the "Create PivotTable" popup menu to begin creating your PivotTable.

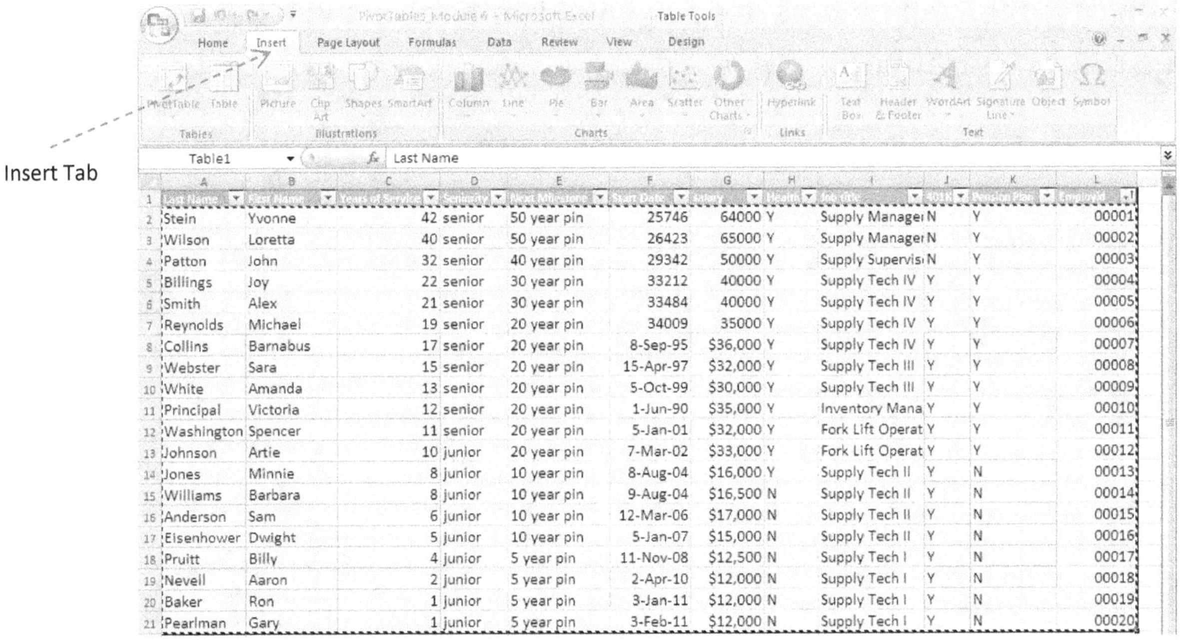

Figure 6-1 Highlighted Excel data table.

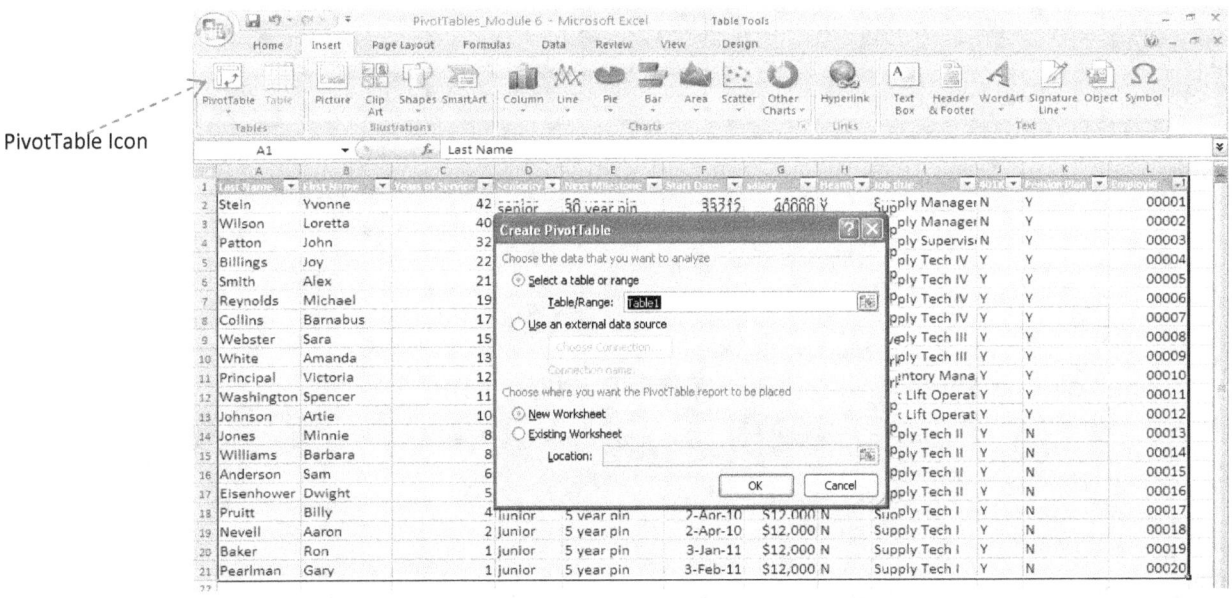

Figure 6-2 Highlighted Excel data table with "Create PivotTable "popup menu

© TopToolsandTraining LLC

63

The PivotTable Field List Task pane and Shell of PivotTable

After selecting, "OK", from the Create PivotTable popup menu, two elements will be displayed. The **PivotTable Field List pane** and **the shell of the PivotTable (figure 6-3)**. The **PivotTable Field List pane** will be used to define the layout and content of the PivotTable Report. The **shell of PivotTable,** will be where your PivotTable report will be displayed once it is defined.

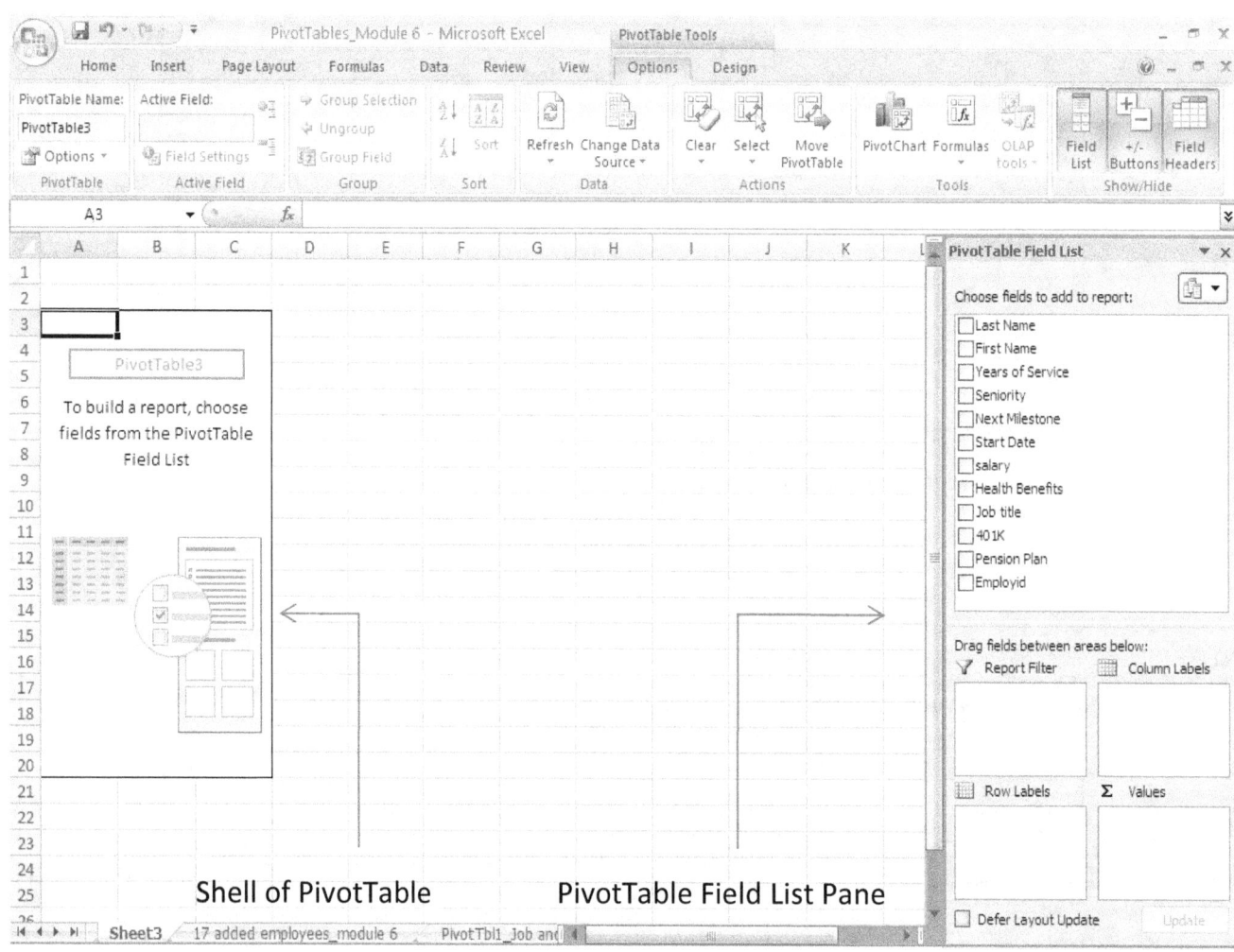

Figure 6-3 Shell of PivotTable and PivotTable Field List Pane.

PivotTable – Data Analysis

Module 6

The PivotTable Field List Task pane Sections

The **PivotTable Field List Task pane** is the MS Excel 2007 feature that is used to define the PivotTable Report (**figure 6-4**). It contains a list of header names (fields), that when selected, make up the content of your PivotTable report. It also contains Area Boxes that are used to define the layout of the PivotTable report.

The PivotTable Field List Task pane is divided into two sections, the Field and Area. The **Field Section** list the fields available in the Excel data. The data from the field names selected will be used to create the PivotTable report. The **Area Section** is use, to define the layout of the Excel data selected and extracted. The Area section consist of the Report Filter, Column Labels, Row Labels and Values boxes.

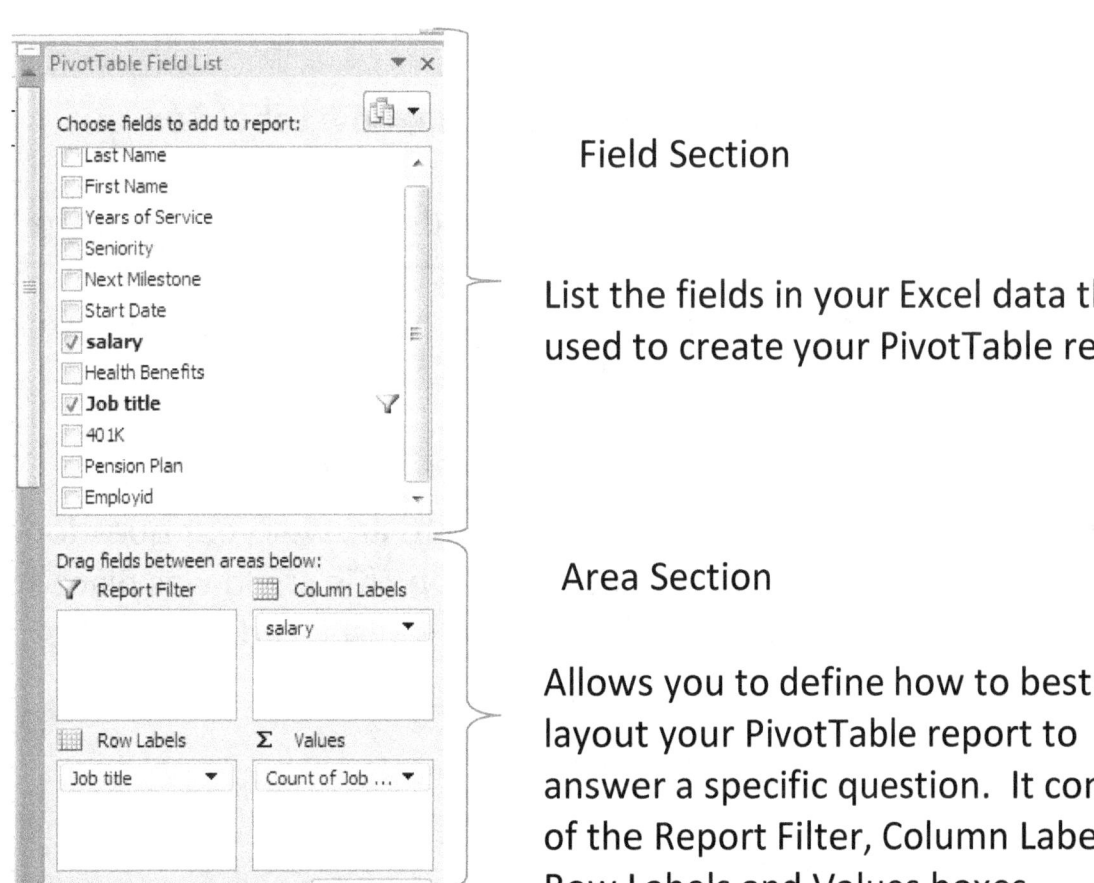

Field Section

List the fields in your Excel data that will be used to create your PivotTable report.

Area Section

Allows you to define how to best layout your PivotTable report to answer a specific question. It consist of the Report Filter, Column Labels, Row Labels and Values boxes.

Figure 6-4 MS Excel 2007 PivotTable Field List pane.

PivotTable – Data Analysis
Module 6

The PivotTable Field List Task pane, Field Section

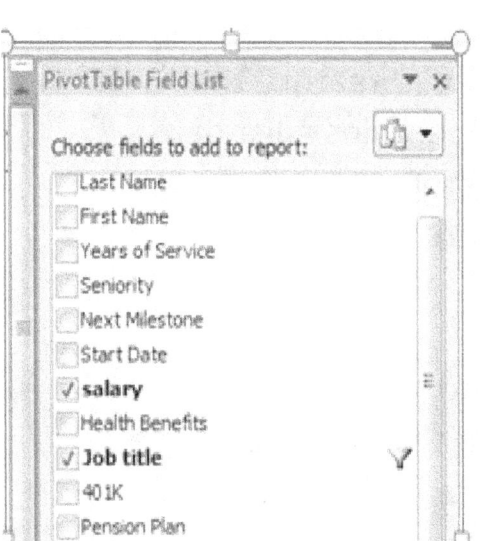

When considering the content of your PivotTable report you should first consider the fields that are relevant to the question being asked. The relevant fields can be chosen from the "Field Section" of the PivotTable Field List pane. They are chosen by putting a check in each required field's check box.

In figure 6-5, you can see the "Salary" and "Job Title" fields were chosen. This is indicated by checks shown in the checkboxes next to the chosen fields (figure 6-5).

Figure 6-5 MS Excel 2007 PivotTable Field List pane with salary and Job Title fields checked.

The PivotTable Field List Task pane, Area Section, Row Label Box

Once you have determined the pivot points (fields needed to answer the question being asked) the values should be selected and placed in the "Row Labels" box (figure 6-6). The "Row Labels" box is located in the Area Section of the PivotTable Field List Task pane.

Remember, the value being placed, in the "Row Labels" box will be the name of the field that contains the data needed to answer your question. In the example shown below (**figure 6-6**), the "Job Title" field was placed in the "Row Labels" box. The "Job Title" data, will be displayed, across the rows of your report.

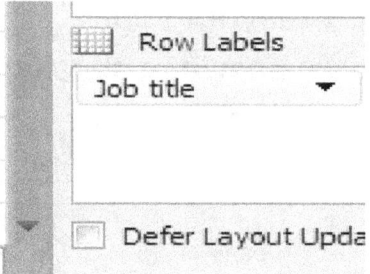

Figure 6-6 MS Excel 2007 PivotTable Field List pane, Area Section, Row Labels box.

PivotTable – Data Analysis
Module 6

The PivotTable Field List Task pane, Area Section, Column Label Box

For simple PivotTables you may only need to populate the Row Labels box with one field. But, for more complex questions, it will be easier to decipher your data if you use both rows and columns.

In the example use for this exercise we will use both rows and columns. In the figure shown below you see the "Salary" field was dragged from the Field List into the Column Labels (**figure 6-7**) box.

Just as the data extracted from the the fields placed in the Row Labels box, the data extracted from the field being placed in the Column Labels box, will also be used to answer your question. It will be displayed across the columns of your PivotTable Report.

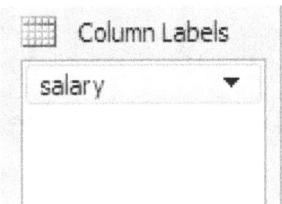

Figure 6-7 MS Excel 2007 PivotTable Field List pane, Area Section, Column Labels box.

PivotTable – Data Analysis
Module 6

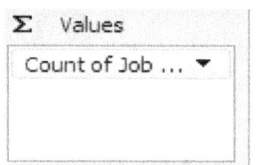

Figure 6-8 MS Excel 2007 PivotTable Field List pane, Area Section's Values box.

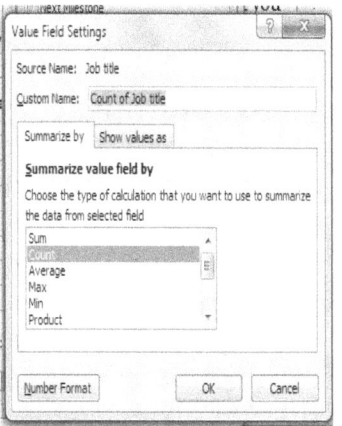

Figure 6-9 MS Excel 2007 PivotTable, Value Field Settings menu.

Figure 6-10 MS Excel 2007 PivotTable Field List pane, Area Section, Report Filter box.

The PivotTable Field List Task pane, Area Section, Values Box

We have described how to select the data and layout of your PivotTable Report. You can now select how you want to summarize the results. To do this you will need to select the field you want to use as the summary criteria. For our example, "Job title" was chosen as the summary criteria. So you would drag "Job title" into the Values box (**figure 6-8**).

Once, you place the "Job title" field in the Values box, Excel will default to a summary setting (i.e. Sum, Count, Average, Product, etc.). In the example shown in figure 6-8, the setting defaulted to, "Count". If the defaulted setting, is not what you want, you can select the drop-down arrow, next to the field listed in the Values box. Then select the "Value Field Settings" option from the list. The "Value Field Settings" menu will appear (**figure 6-9**). At this point you can choose the summary setting Count, Average, Min, etc.), that will satisfy your requirements.

The PivotTable Field List Task pane, Area Section, Report Filter Box

Finally, if the fields that you placed in the Row Labels and/or Column Labels box(es) require further filtering, then the Report Filter box (**figure 6-10**) can be used.

You can accomplish this by dragging a field value from the field list into the Report Filter box.

Remember, the field, being placed, in the Report Filter box, will be your method of further filtering the data. The filtered dat, will appear in the rows or columns (pivot points) of your PivotTable.

PivotTable Creation Exercise

Through the use of the Employee data table that was created in our earlier exercise you will now explore the use of the PivotTable features in Excel.

Scenario #4: The ACME parts department was merged with another department, and now has 20 employees (**figure 6-11**). The Director of the ACME parts department is trying to get his arms around what he now owns. His goal is to better manage his personnel.

The ACME Part Director requested a report that provides specific **Job title** and **Salary** information. The type of information that he is trying to obtain is the number or **count** of resources assigned to each Job title, along with their salaries. The actual phrasing, of his question was, "Can you provide me a report that list my employee's Job Titles and associated salaries?" He also wants to know the number of employees, in each "Job title".

Remember, your first step, in creating a PivotTable report is to identify the pivot point. Ask yourself, "What question(s) are you being asked to answer?". As you ponder the manager's request, you should recognize the following question, *"what are employees Job Titles?"*. Therefore, one of the fields, that points, to the data needed, will be, "Job titles". You should also see, the question, *"what are the salaries for each Job title?"*. So, the second required field will be "Salary". So, you now know that you will require two fields, (1) "Job title" and (2) "Salary".

Next, you should ask yourself, "how does the manager, want the answer summarized or grouped?". Well, lets take another look at the ACME Parts Director's, question. The ACME Parts Director asked, "... *how many employees,* are in each, "Job title", and what are their salaries?". So, it is understood, the ACME Parts Director, wants to summarize, "Job Title", by, "how many" (COUNT) employees, are in each. So, the summary criteria, is **COUNT** of Job titles.

PivotTable – Data Analysis
Module 6

Added Seventeen additional employee's data to the data table.

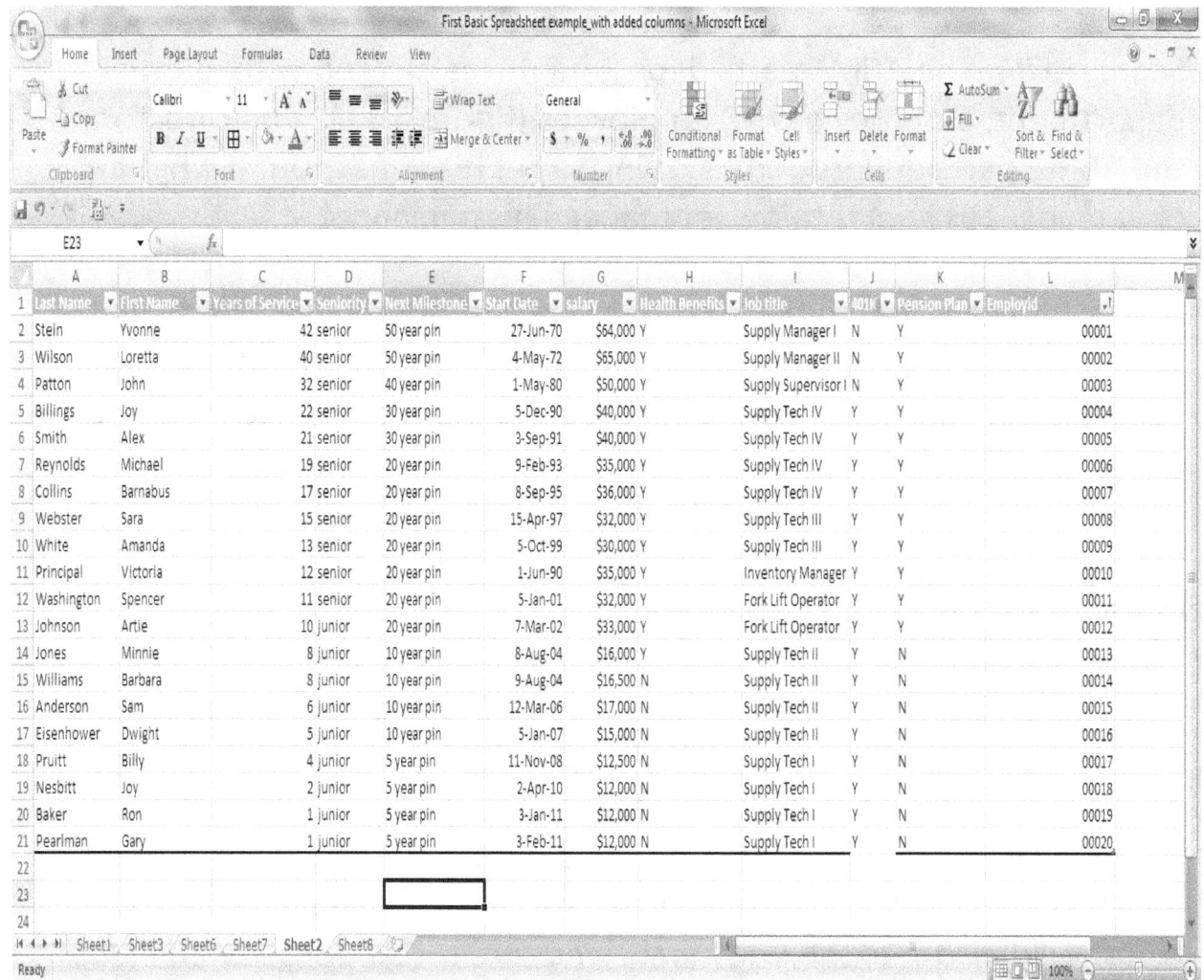

Figure 6-11 MS Excel 2007 Data Table with the seventeen additional employees.

*Access the "**PivotTables_module6.xlsx**" from the CD that came with this manual to see hands-on examples, 17 employees data table; PivotTbl1_Job and Salry_mod 6; PivotTbl1_Job and Salry by Row; and PivotTbl2_YrofSvc_Salry_mod 6 ; PivotTbl3_YrofSvc_Over30_Mod6*

PivotTable – Data Analysis
Module 6

Creating a PivotTable Report – Scenario 4

You will now create a PivotTable, using the employee tracking data table, you created, in the previous module.

1) Place your cursor on any cell in your employee tracking data table and click once, by pressing your left mouse button.
2) Next, select the Insert tab from the Ribbon Interface.
3) Within, the "Tables" group on the Insert tab select the PivotTable icon. The, "create PivotTable" popup, will appear.
As you can see, your Table name will appear in the Table/Range field.
4) Select, the "OK" button on the bottom right of the pop-up.
A new worksheet will be created. You will see the shell of the PivotTable, and the PivotTable Field List, on the new worksheet (figure 6-12). Also, you will see a new tab labeled, "Options"*.

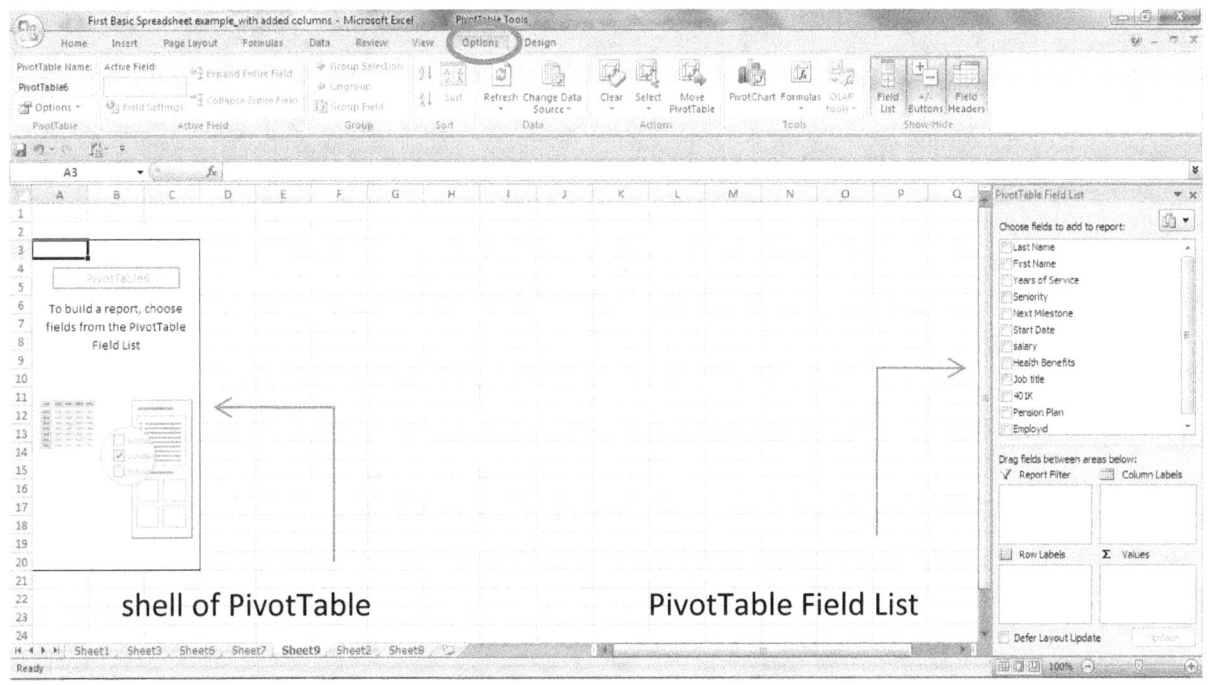

Figure 6-12 MS Excel 2007 worksheet with PivotTable Field List and shell of PivotTable.

* Since you created a PivotTable object in our spreadsheet you are provided a **contextual tab**. As discussed in module 5.

You will start your PivotTable by selecting the check boxes, for "Job Title" and "Salary". These are the two fields, that you identified to answer the ACME Parts Director's, question. As you can see, in figure 6-13, checks are in the check boxes for each of these fields.

As you can also see, Excel assumed (defaulted) you wanted "Job Title", in the Row Labels box and "Salary", in the Values box. So, it placed them there. This led to the creation of a PivotTable, that displays, the sum of the salaries, associated with each "Job title" (fig. 6-13). This is not what you wanted!

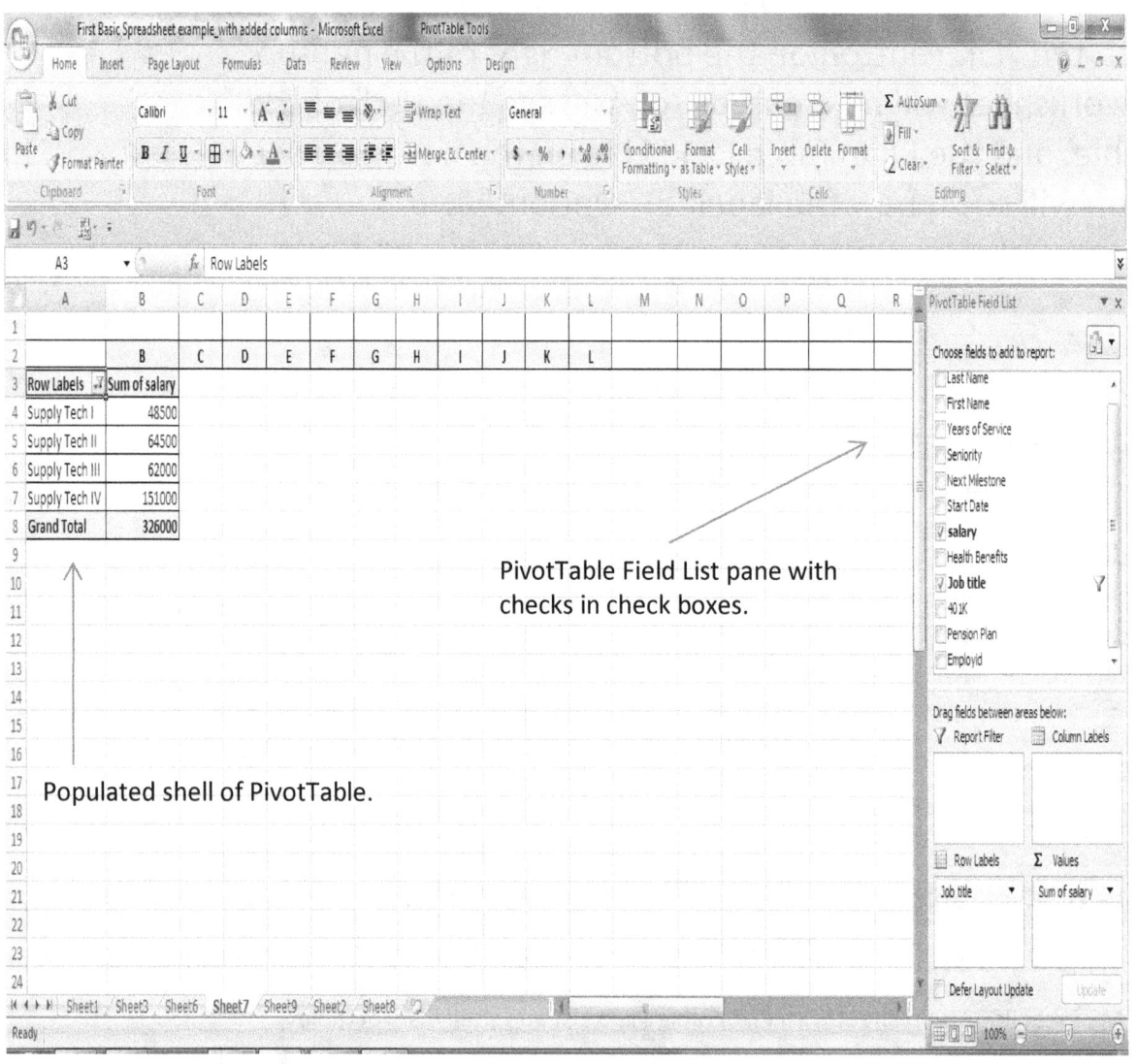

Figure 6-13 MS Excel worksheet with PivotTable.

PivotTable – Data Analysis

Module 6

Steps to creating a PivotTable Report, that displays, <u>Number of employees per job title with their associated salaries</u>.

You can correct Excel's layout assumption by,

1) placing the cursor on top of the "Salary" field located in the Values Box (**figure 6-14**).
2) Press the left mouse button and hold it.
3) Next, drag the "Salary" field up to the Column Labels box, then release the left mouse button (**figure 6-15**).
4) Next, place the mouse over the "Job title" field located in the Field List Box.
5) Press, the left mouse button and hold it.
6) Next, drag the "Job Title" field to the Values box then release the left mouse button (**figure 6-15**).

Before

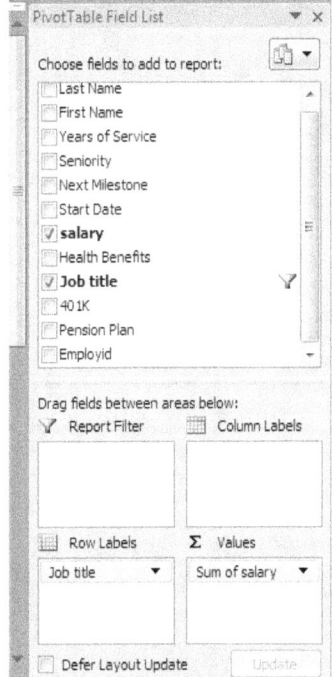

Figure 6-14 MS Excel 2007 PivotTable Field List with "Job Title" field in Row Labels box and the "Sum of Salary" in the Values box.

After

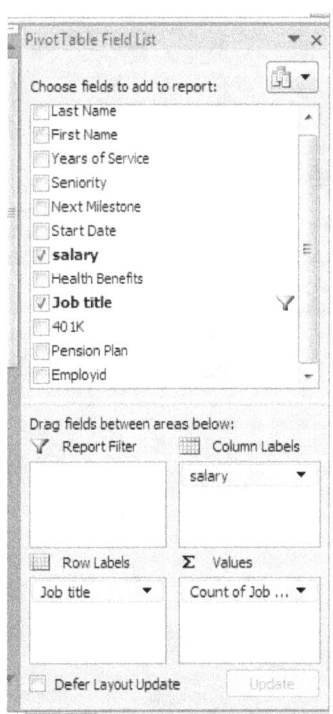

Figure 6-15 MS Excel 2007 PivotTable Field List with "Job Title" field in Row Labels box, "Salary" in the Column Labels box the "count of Job title" in the Values box.

PivotTable – Data Analysis
Module 6

Scenario 4– Solution

You now have a PivotTable that shows all nine "Job titles", in Rows A5 thru A13. It also shows, "Salary", in columns B - P. In order for the ACME Parts Director to interpret the data he'll need to read across the rows, from left to right. Looking across each row, he'll be able to see how many employees (Count) are assigned to a "Job title". He'll also see, the "Salary" of the employee's assigned to that "Job title". In the example shown in **figure 6-16**, row 5 shows the Fork Lift Operator job title has 2 employees assigned. Their salaries, are, $32000 and $33000. Also note, the grand total, of the number of employees, associated to each Job title, is shown in the last column.

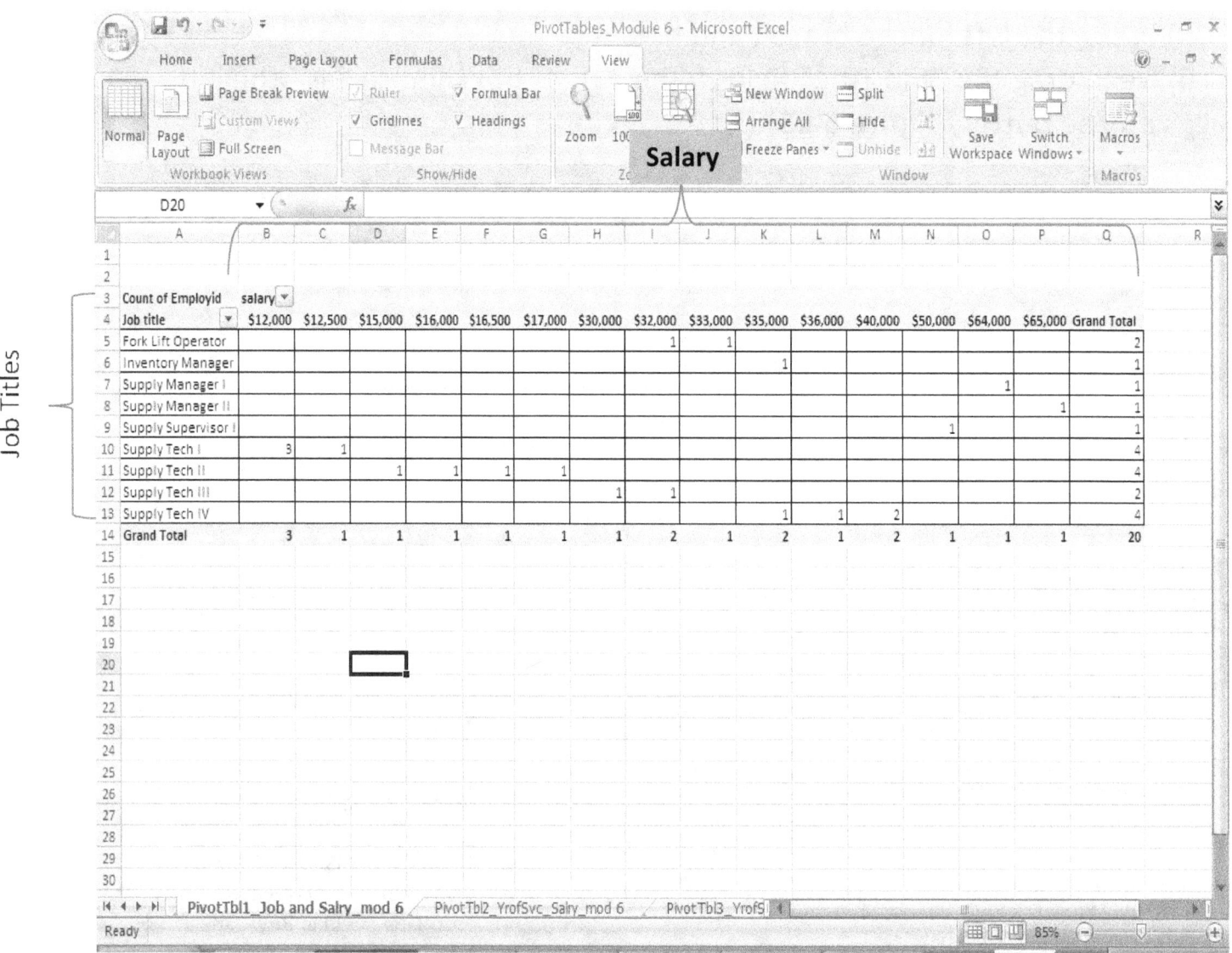

Figure 6-16 MS Excel worksheet with PivotTable.

PivotTable Report displayed using only Rows

As stated earlier you have the option to display your answer using rows only, or rows and columns. We will now use the same data from Scenario 3 to demonstrate using Rows only. Instead of placing, the "Salary" field, in the Columns Label box, you will place it in the Row Labels box along with "Job Title" (see **Figure 6-17**).

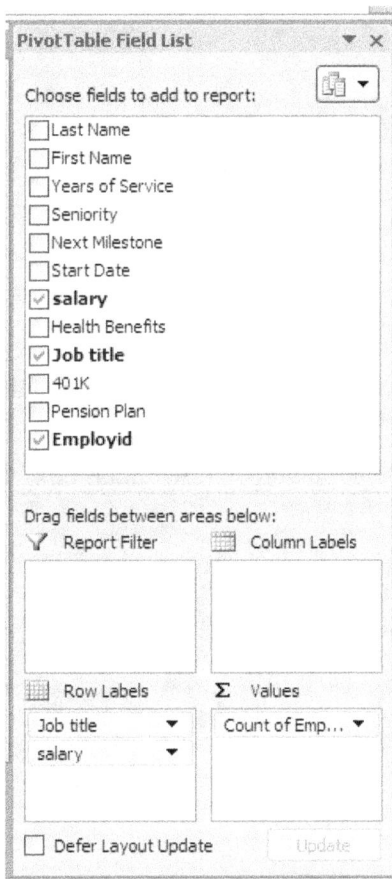

Figure 6-17 MS Excel worksheet 2007 PivotTable Field List

In **figures 6-18,** you have the same data that was displayed in **figure 6-16.** Except, the answer is displayed by rows only. To see the salary information for each Job title, you must expand the row by clicking on the plus sign next to the Job title name (**figure 6-19**). Also, note the summary information (Count of employees) is shown in column B. As you can see, in Figure 6-19 (expanded view), the Fork Lift Operator Job title is assigned to two employees. Their salaries, are $32,000 and $33,000.

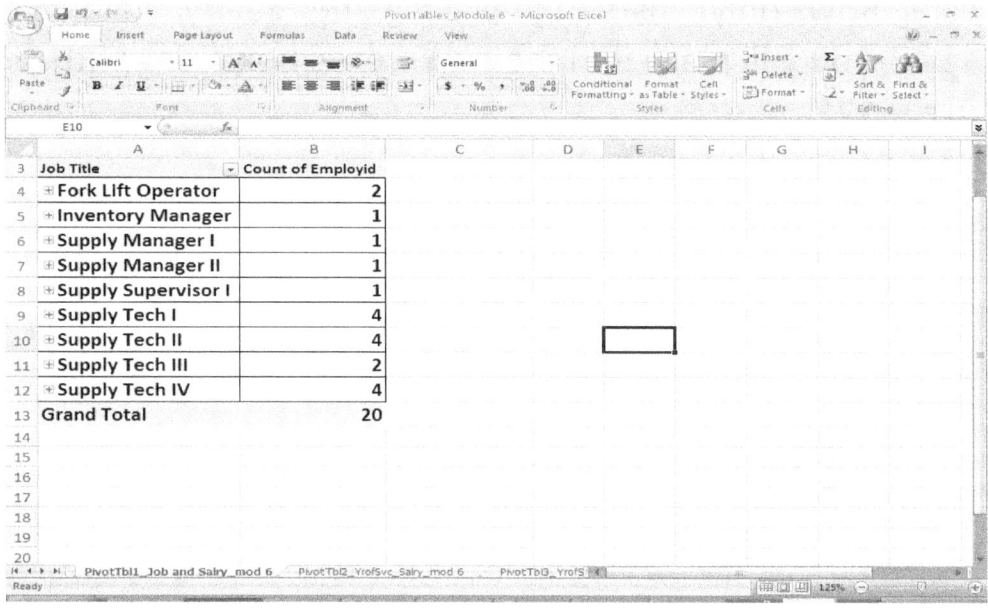

Figure 6-18 PivotTable with all field values populated in Row Labels box (rows condensed).

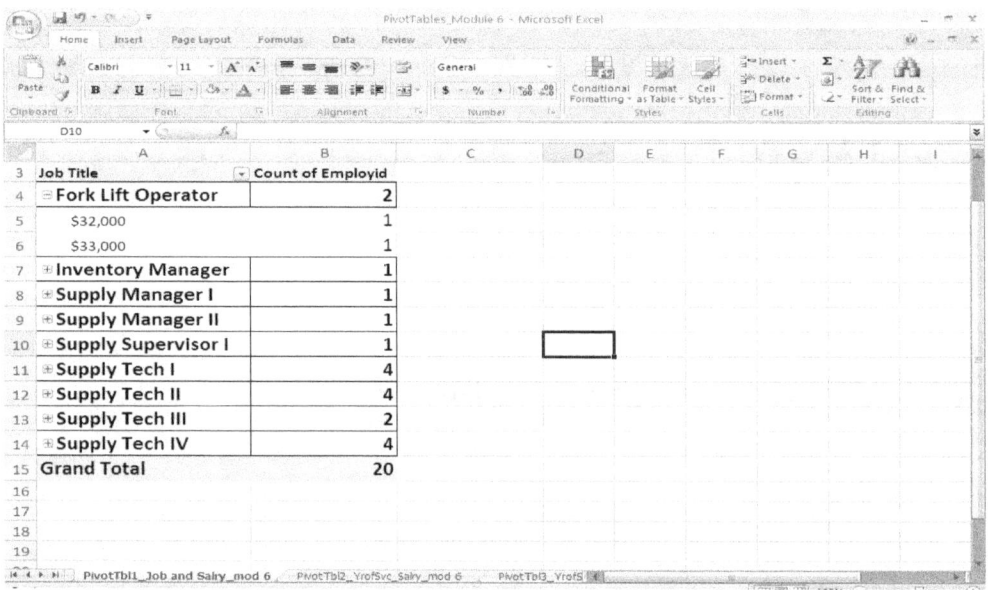

Figure 6-19 PivotTable with all field values populated in Row Labels box (rows expanded).

PivotTable – Data Analysis
Module 6

Creating a PivotTable Report – Scenario 5

Lets try, a few more examples to gain a firm grasp of PivotTables.

Scenario #5: The ACME Parts Director has another request. He wants to know, the **count** of employees, by **years of service** and **salary**.

We will start with a fresh worksheet. Go to the previously used PivotTable Field List Task pane. Uncheck all fields in the Field list. Your worksheet should look exactly like the one shown below (**figure 6-20**).

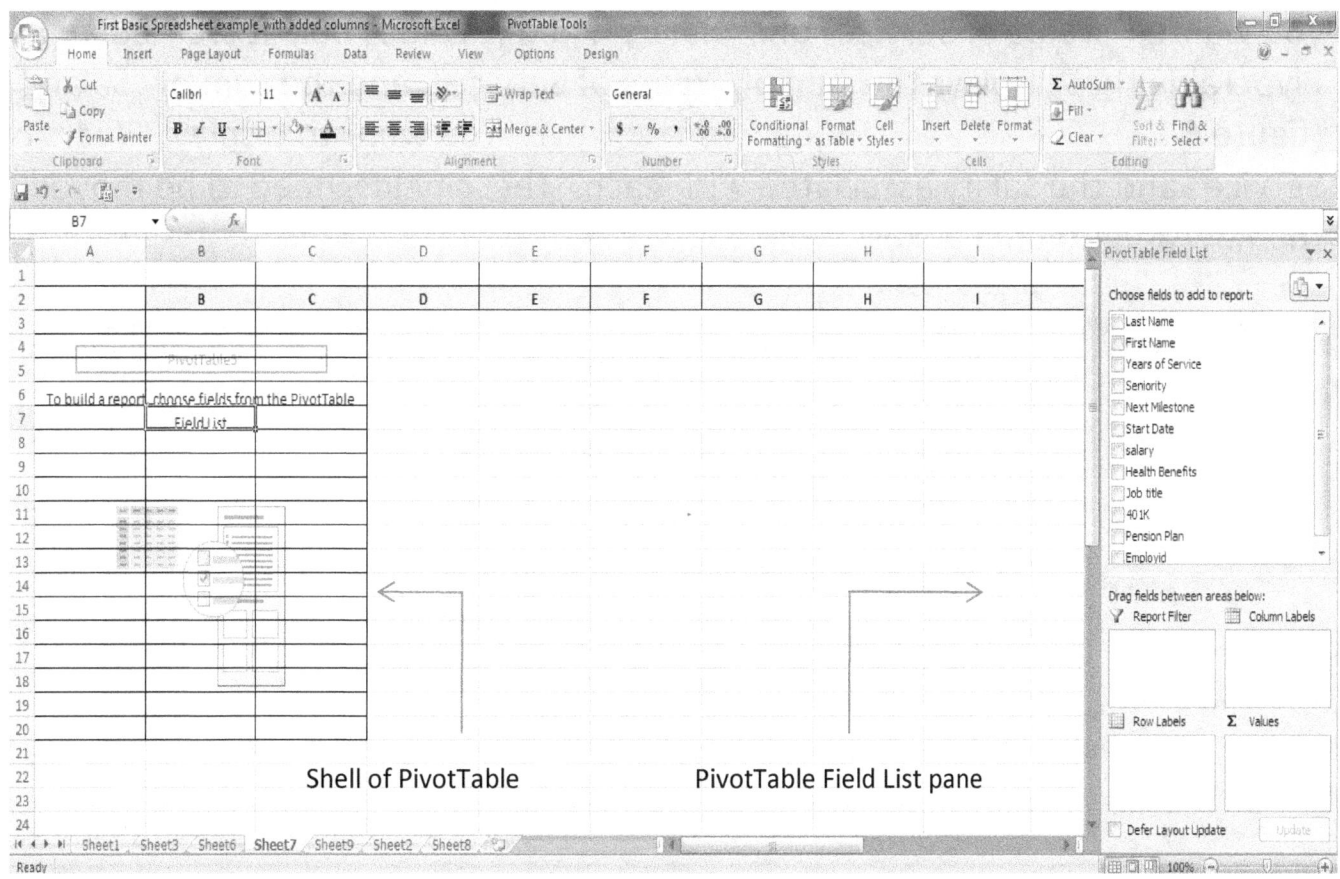

Figure 6-20 MS Excel 2007 worksheet with PivotTable Field List and shell of PivotTable.

TopToolsandTraining LLC

PivotTable – Data Analysis

Module 6

First, reflect on "what you are being asked to answer?". Answer: You are being asked to identify employees by "Years of Service" and "Salary". The next question to be considered is, "how to summarize the data?" Answer: Number of employees (count), by Years of Service, and salary.

So, based on our earlier discussion, the fields needed to answer the manager's question will be placed in the Row Labels and Columns Labels boxes. And the count of employees, per salary, and Years of Service, will be a field placed in the Values Box.

You will start, your PivotTable by selecting the check boxes for "Years of Service" and "Salary". The check boxes for each field, are shown in the PivotTable Field List Task pane. As you can see, when you selected the two fields Excel assumed you wanted "Years of Service" and "Salary", in the Values box. It created a PivotTable that displays the sum of "Years of Service", and the sum of "Salary" (**figure 6-21**). Excel's assumption was incorrect! You want to display, "Years of Service" and the salary associated with each. These fields, need to be moved, to the Row and Column boxes.

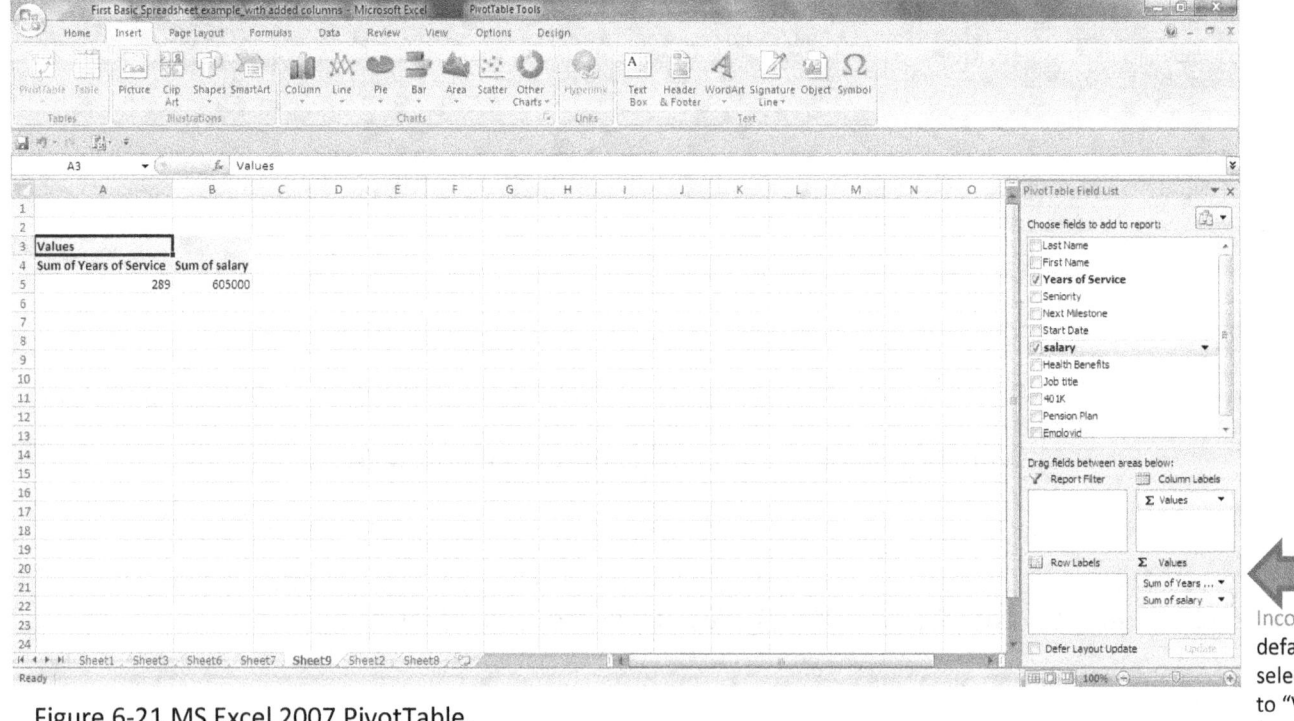

Figure 6-21 MS Excel 2007 PivotTable.

Incorrectly defaulted the selected fields to "Values" box..

78

TopToolsandTraining LLC

Steps to creating a PivotTable Report, that displays, <u>Employee Years of Service and the salary associated with each.</u>

You can correct Excel's default layout assumption by,

1) placing the cursor on top of the "Years of Service" field located in the Values Box.
2) Next, press the left mouse button and hold it.
3) Drag, the "Years of Service" field over to the Row Labels box, then release the left mouse button.
4) Next, place the mouse over the "Salary" field located in the Values Box.
5) Press, the left mouse button and hold it.
6) Next, drag the "Salary" field, to the Column Labels box and release the left mouse button.
7) Next, place the mouse over the "Years of Service" field located in the Field List Box.
8) Next, press the left mouse button and hold it.
9) Next, drag the "Years of Service" field to the Values box then release the left mouse button.
10) Note: Excel defaulted the formula in the Values box to "Sum". This is not correct. You want a Count.
11) So, you must now select the drop-down arrowhead located on the top right of the Values Box.
12) Next, select "Value Field Setting" from the menu.
13) Select, "Count", from the Value Field Settings menu then select the "OK" button located on the bottom right of the Value Field Settings pop-up.

PivotTable – Data Analysis
Module 6

Scenario 5 – Solution

You now have a PivotTable, that shows all "Years of Service", in Rows A5 thru A22 (**figure 6-22**). It also shows, "Salary", in columns B- P. In order for the ACME Parts Director to interpret the data, he will look across the rows left to right. Looking across each row it is easy to see "Years of Service", and the number employees, in each salary level. Row 5, can be interpreted, as 2 employees, with 1 year of service and their annual salaries are $12,000 each. Row 10, shows 2 employees with 8 years of service and their annual salaries are, $16,000 and $16,500, respectively.

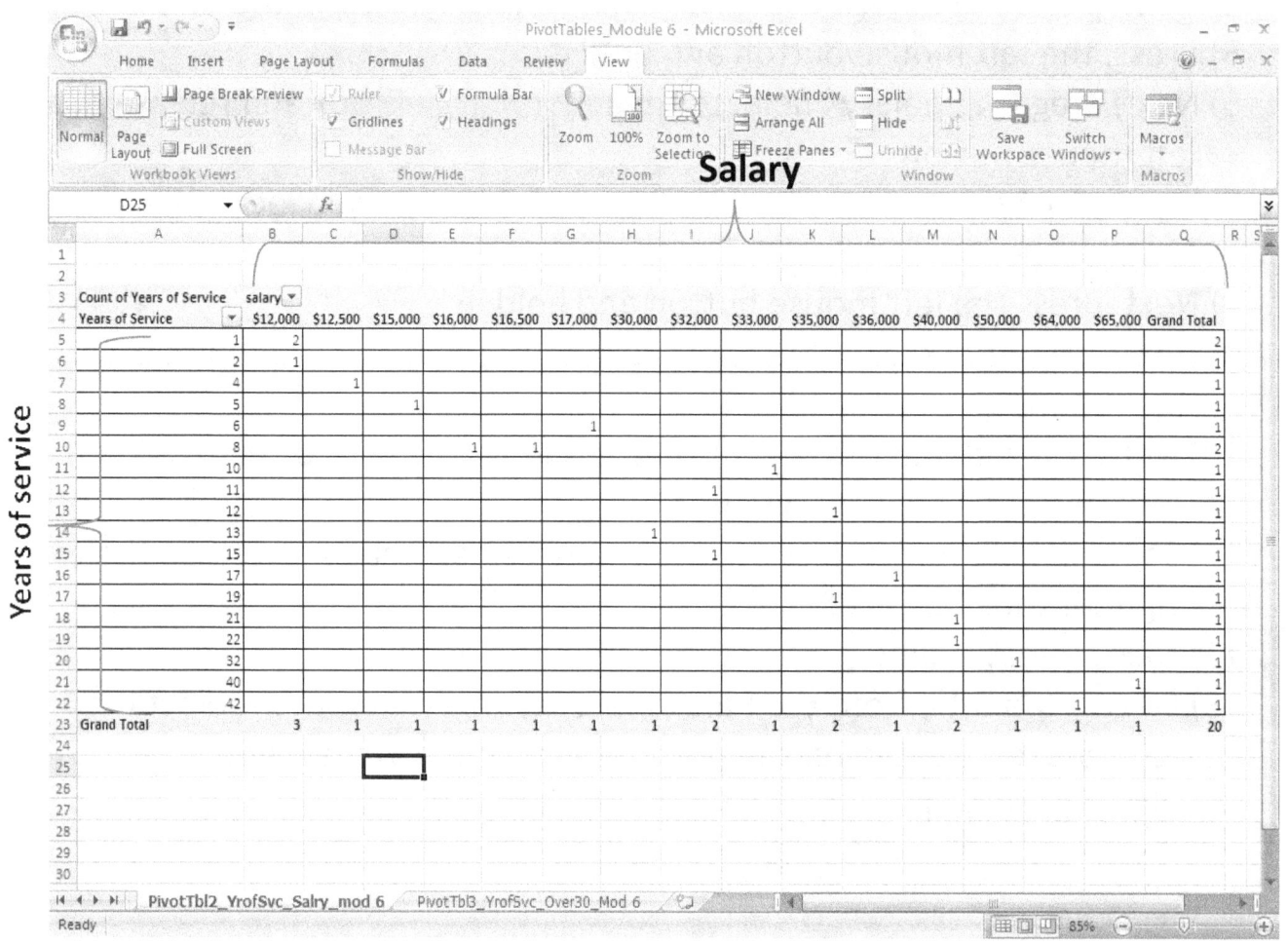

Figure 6-22 PivotTable displaying Count of Employees by Years of Service and Salary.

Filtering a PivotTable Report – Scenario 6

Scenario #6: After reviewing, the salary range, for "Years of Service", the ACME parts Director requested, the "Job Title", and Count of employees who have "Years of Service", over 30.

Steps to creating a PivotTable Report that displays, <u>Salary and Job title of all employees with over 30 years of service.</u>

Since you are now pretty good, at creating PivotTables, you know that you need to:

1) drag, "Years of Service", from the Fields List to the Row Labels box.
2) Next, go to the "Years of Service" drop-down arrow `Years of Service ▼` , located on the top of the PivotTable.
3) Click, the "Select All" check box, located on the "Select Field" popup menu (this will clear all checks).
4) Now, select, 32, 40 and 42, from the "Select Field" pop-up menu.
5) Select, the "OK" button located on the bottom left of the "Select Field" pop-up menu.
6) Next, drag "salary" into the Column Labels box".
7) Finally, drag "Job title", from the Fields List to the Values box. This will define how data is to be summarized.

Scenario 6 – Solution - Filtered PivotTable Report

You now have a PivotTable that has been filtered for specific "Years of Service". This is shown in cells B4, C4, and D4. It also shows, the "Job Title" associated with the specified, "Years of Service". This is shown in cells A5 thru A7. And it shows the count of resources holding those job titles as they relate, to the "years of service". Shown, in cells B7, C6, and D5.

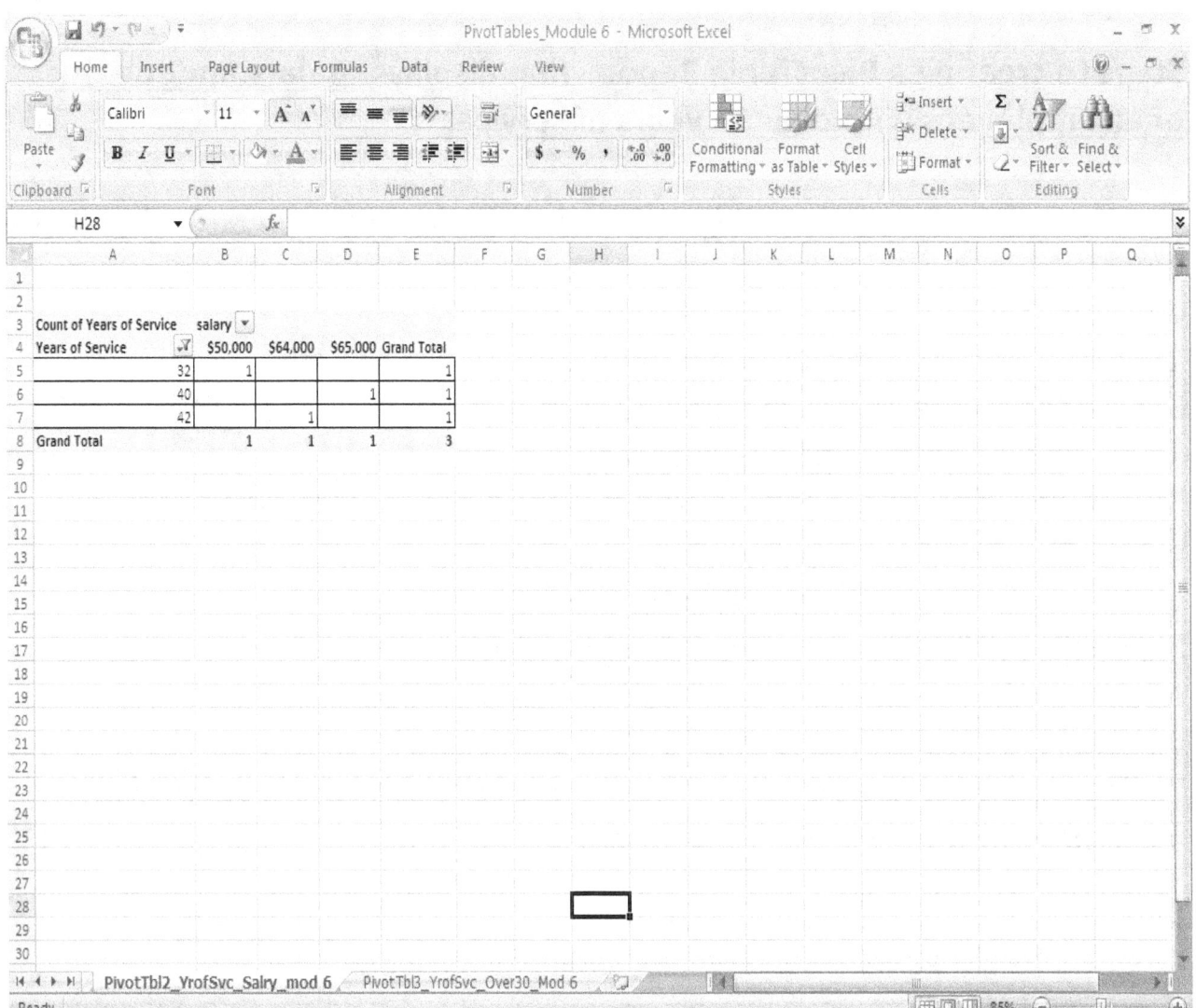

Figure 6-23 Filtered PivotTable displaying Count of Employees by Years of Service and Salary.

What have you learned so far?

1) What is a PivotTable.
2) What questions, to ask yourself, before you create, a PivotTable.
3) How to create a PivotTable, from a data table, using a function, located in the Insert tab.
4) How to access the PivotTable Field List Task Pane.
5) How to use the Field List, Row Label, Column Label and Value Boxes, within, the PivotTable Field List Task Pane.
6) How to interpret PivotTable results.
7) How to add, field data, to an existing PivotTable.
8) How to filter data in a PivotTable.

Module 7

CHARTS AND GRAPHS
TRENDS IN DATA

As was explained in the last module, PivotTables provide you the ability to better answer questions about your Excel data. As you will see in this module, an effective method to further clarify your answer can be pictures and charts.

In this module you will create charts from PivotTable data.

Scenario #7: The ACME Parts Director was tasked to provide his upper Management an executive presentation explaining the (1) size of his organization; (2) annual resource cost; (3) cost by job title; and (4) years of service of each individual in his organization.

The ACME Parts Director opts to provide this information as charts. So, of course, he assigns this task to you. Since you **are** the Excel expert.

Access the "PivotTables_module7.xlsx" from the CD that came with this manual to to see hands-on examples PivotChart 1_module 7, PivotChart 2_module 7, PivotChart 3_module 7 and PivotChart 4_module 7 .

First, lets review, what the ACME Parts Director is requesting.

- A chart that explains the size of ACME Parts Department (count of employees). – Chart 1

- A chart that explains the ACME Parts Department's annual resource cost. - Chart 2

- A chart that explains the ACME Parts Department's cost, by job role or title. - Chart 3

- A chart that explains the Job title and years of service for each employee in ACME's Parts Department. – Chart 4

Creating shell of PivotTable and PivotTable Field List Pane

You will now create a PivotTable using the employee tracking data table you created in the previous module.

1) Place your cursor on any cell in your Employee Tracking Data Table and click once, by pressing your left mouse button.
2) Next, select the "Insert" tab from the Ribbon Interface.
3) Within, the **Tables** group on the "**Insert**" tab, select the PivotChart icon. The, "create PivotTable with PivotChart", popup will appear.
As you can see, your Table name, will appear in the Table/Range field.
4) Select, the "OK" button, on the bottom right of the pop-up.
A new work sheet will be created. You will see the shell of the PivotTable and the PivotTable Field List on the new worksheet (**figure 7-1**). Also, you will see a PivotChart Filter pane.

Charts and Graphs
Module 7

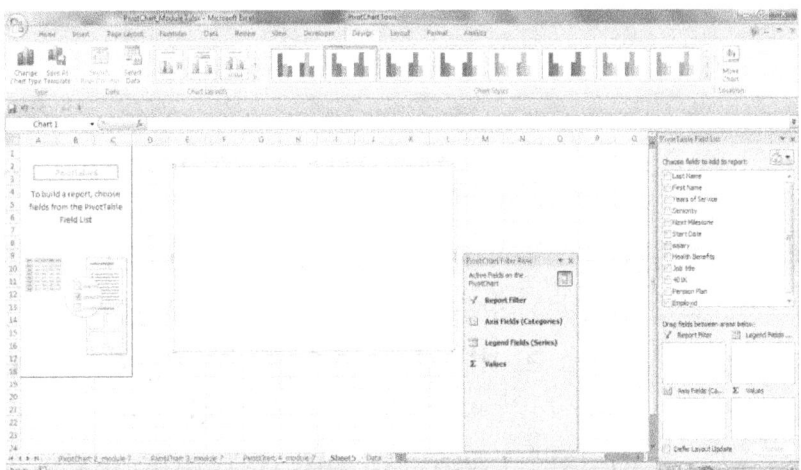

Figure 7-1 MS Excel 2007 worksheet with shell of PivotTable and PivotTable Field List.

Defining requirements for Size of ACME Parts Department (Chart 1)

First, consider what is being requested? The answer, "Count of employees". Therefore, applying what you learned in the previous module, you place the "Employid" field in the Values Box.

You will start your PivotChart by selecting the "EmployId" check box, located in the PivotTable Field List Task pane.

As you can see, when you selected "EmployId", Excel assumed you wanted it placed in the Values box. It created a PivotTable that displays, the sum of the "EmployId".

Note: Excel, defaulted the summary method, in the Values box, to **Sum**. This is not correct. We want a **Count**.

Changing the summary method in the Values box from Sum to Count.

1) To correct the summary method, select the drop-down arrow located on the top right, of the Values box.
2) Next, select "Value Field Setting...", from the menu.
3) Finally, from the Value Field settings menu, select "Count". Next, click the "OK" button shown on the bottom right of the "Value Field settings" pop-up.
4) You now have the correct PivotTable.

Creating Chart 1 - Size of ACME Parts Department (count of employees)

As stated earlier, along with your chart, a PivotChart Filter Pane popup will be displayed (see fig 7-2, below). This pane displays the fields that you populated in the PivotTable Field List pane. These identified fields will be used to create your chart. In figure 7-2, the PivotChart Filter Pane shows that the Values boxof the PivotTable field list pane was populated with "Count of Employid".

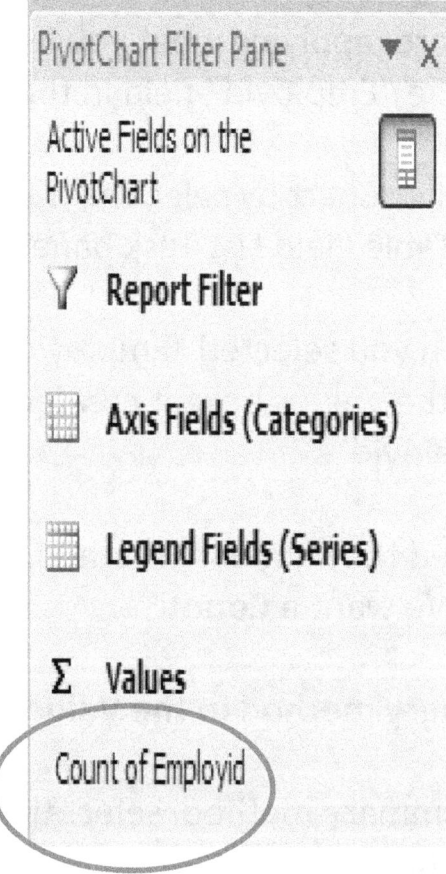

Figure 7-2 PivotChart Filter pane.

Adding a Title Name to Chart 1 - Size of ACME Parts Department

To make your chart, easy for the executives to interpret, you will rename the title of this chart. This is accomplished by:

1) closing the PivotChart Filter pane, by selecting the "x", in the top right corner .
2) Next, place your cursor on the chart title "Total", shown at the top of your newly created chart.
3) Next, press your left mouse button once, to access the title text box.
4) Next, type "Number of Employees in ACME Parts Department" in the title text box.
5) Now, select the "Layout" tab from the Ribbon Interface.
6) Select, the "Axes" icon from the "Axes group".
7) Select, "Primary Horizontal Axis title" then select from the pop-up menu, "None".
8) Next, select the "Axis title" icon from the "Labels group".
9) Select, "Primary Horizontal Axis title" then select from the pop-up menu, "Title Below Axis". *A text box will appear below your horizontal axis.*
10) Type "Employee(s)" in the Title Axis text box.
11) Next, select the "Axis title" icon from the "Labels group".
12) Select, "Primary Vertical Axis title" then select from the pop-up menu, "Rotated Title". *A rotated text box will appear next to your vertical axis.*
13) Type "Count" in the Axis text box.

Charts and Graphs

Module 7

Chart 1 – Size of ACME Parts Department (count of employees)

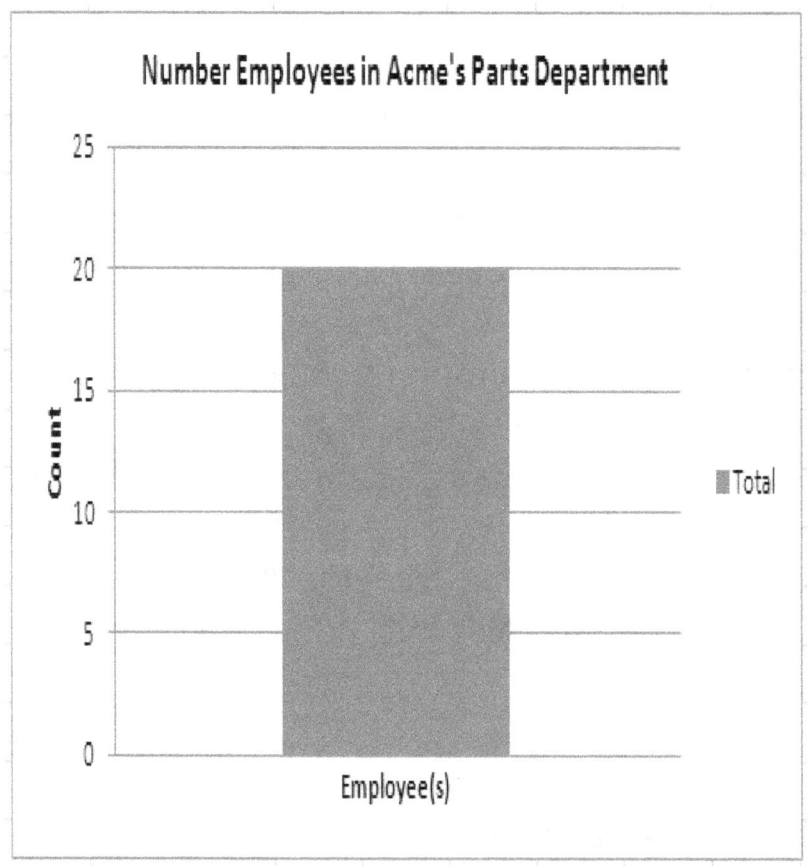

Figure 7-3   PivotChart – Size of in Acme's Part Department. (count of employees)

Satisfied requirements for Chart 1: Number employees in ACME Parts dept.

Charts and Graphs
Module 7

Chart 2 - ACME Parts Department annual resource cost (sum of salaries)

You can now create Chart2. Again, consider what is being requested? The ACME Parts Director is requesting a chart that provides the "Sum of employees annual salary".

You will refresh the PivotTable used in the last exercise by clearing the check from the "employid " check box. Now, select the "Salary" check box located in the PivotTable Field List Task pane.

As you can see, when you selected the "Salary" check box, Excel assumed you wanted it placed in the Values box. It created a PivotChart that displays the sum of the Salaries (see figure 7-4).

Note: Excel defaulted to **Sum,** in the Values box. This is exactly what you wanted. You now have the correct PivotChart.

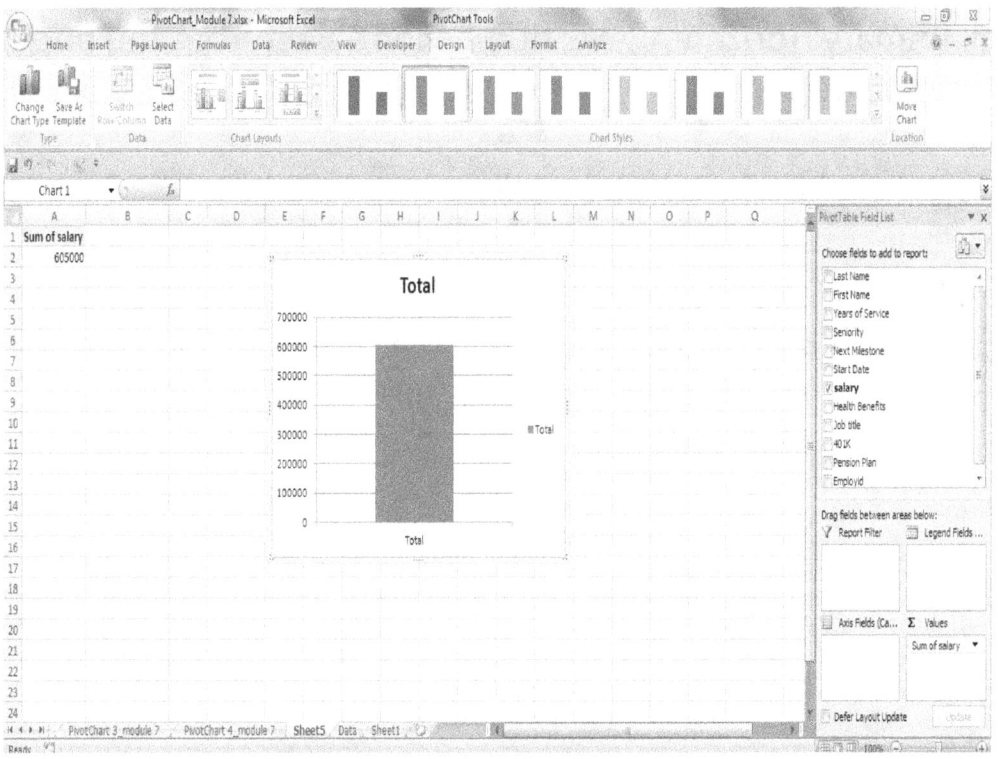

Figure 7-4 MS Excel 2007 Insert tab and Charts group

TopToolsandTraining LLC

Adding a Title Name to Chart 2 - ACME Parts Department Annual Resource Cost (sum of salaries)

Now, to make your chart easy for the executive to interpret, you will rename the title of this chart. This is accomplished by,

1) placing your cursor on "Total" shown at the top of your newly created chart.
2) Next, press your left mouse button once to access the title.
3) Next, type "ACME Parts Department Annual Salary Costs".
4) Now, select the "Layout" tab from the Ribbon Interface.
5) Select, the "Axes" icon from the "Axes group".
6) Select, "Primary Horizontal Axis title" then select from the pop-up menu, "None".
7) Next, select the "Axis title" icon from the "Labels group".
8) Select, "Primary Horizontal Axis title", then select from the pop-up menu, "Title Below Axis". *A text box will appear below your horizontal axis.*
10)   Type "Salary" in the Axis text box.
11)   Next, select the "Axis title" icon from the "Labels group".
12) Select, "Primary Vertical Axis title"then select from the pop-up menu, "Rotated Title". *A rotated text box will appear next to your vertical axis.*
13)   Type "US Currency" in the Axis text box.

Chart 2 - ACME Parts Department annual salary cost (sum of employees salaries)

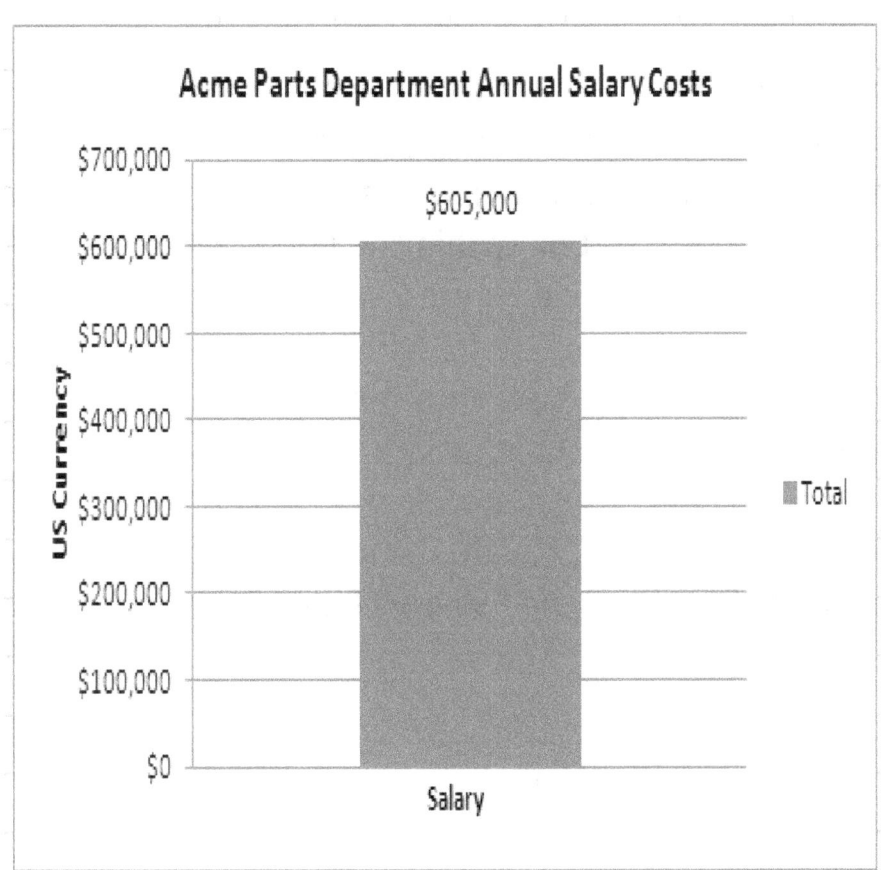

Figure 7-5 PivotChart – ACME Parts Department annual salary costs.

Satisfied requirements for Chart 2: ACME Parts dept annual salary costs.

Chart 3 - ACME Parts Department cost by job role or title

So far, so good. Next, you will create Chart 3. Remember, you must first consider, what question, are you being asked to answer? The ACME Parts Director asked, "What are the sum of salaries associated with each Job Title?" You can tell by the question, the "Job title" and "Salary", are the key fields, to be used.

Populating PivotTable Field List to create a PivotChart

In this example, the "Job Title", will be the field, placed in the Axis Fields box. **Note:** When creating PivotCharts, the name of the Row Labels box located in the PivotTable Field list has changed to Axis Fields. Also, the name of the Column Labels box within the PivotTable Field list has changed to Legend Fields. (See Figure 7-6)

The "Sum of salaries" will be how your results will be summarized. So, you will place the "Salary" field in the Values box.

(**Note:** If you were asked to provide the individual salary of each Job title, you would have placed the "Salary" field in the Legend Fields box.)

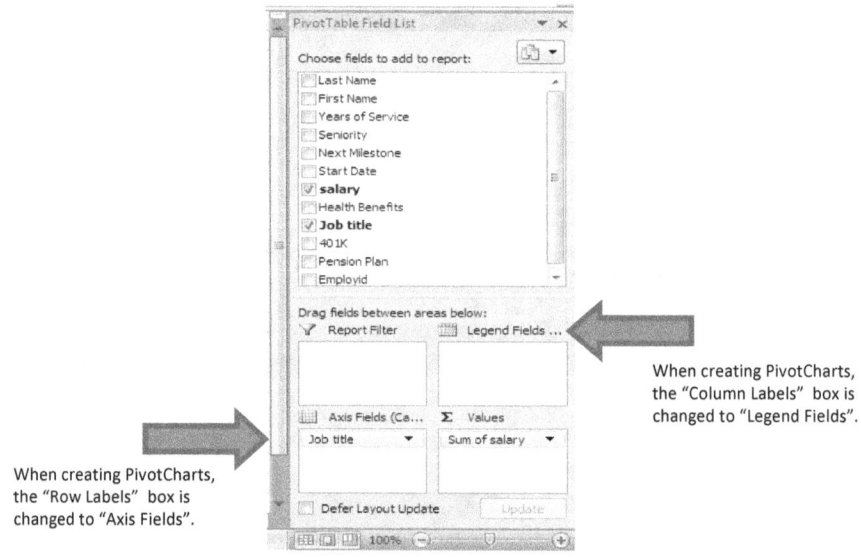

Figure 7-6 PivotTable Filed List – Row Labels box renamed Axis Fields and Column Labels box renamed Legend Fields when used for PivotChart purposes.

Adding a Title Name to Chart 3 - ACME Parts Department cost by job role or title

Now, to make your chart easy for the executive to interpret, you will rename the title of this chart. This is accomplished by,

1) placing your cursor on the Title Text box, shown at the top of your newly created chart.
2) Next, press your left mouse button once to access the title.
3) Next, type "ACME Parts Department Annual Costs by Job title".

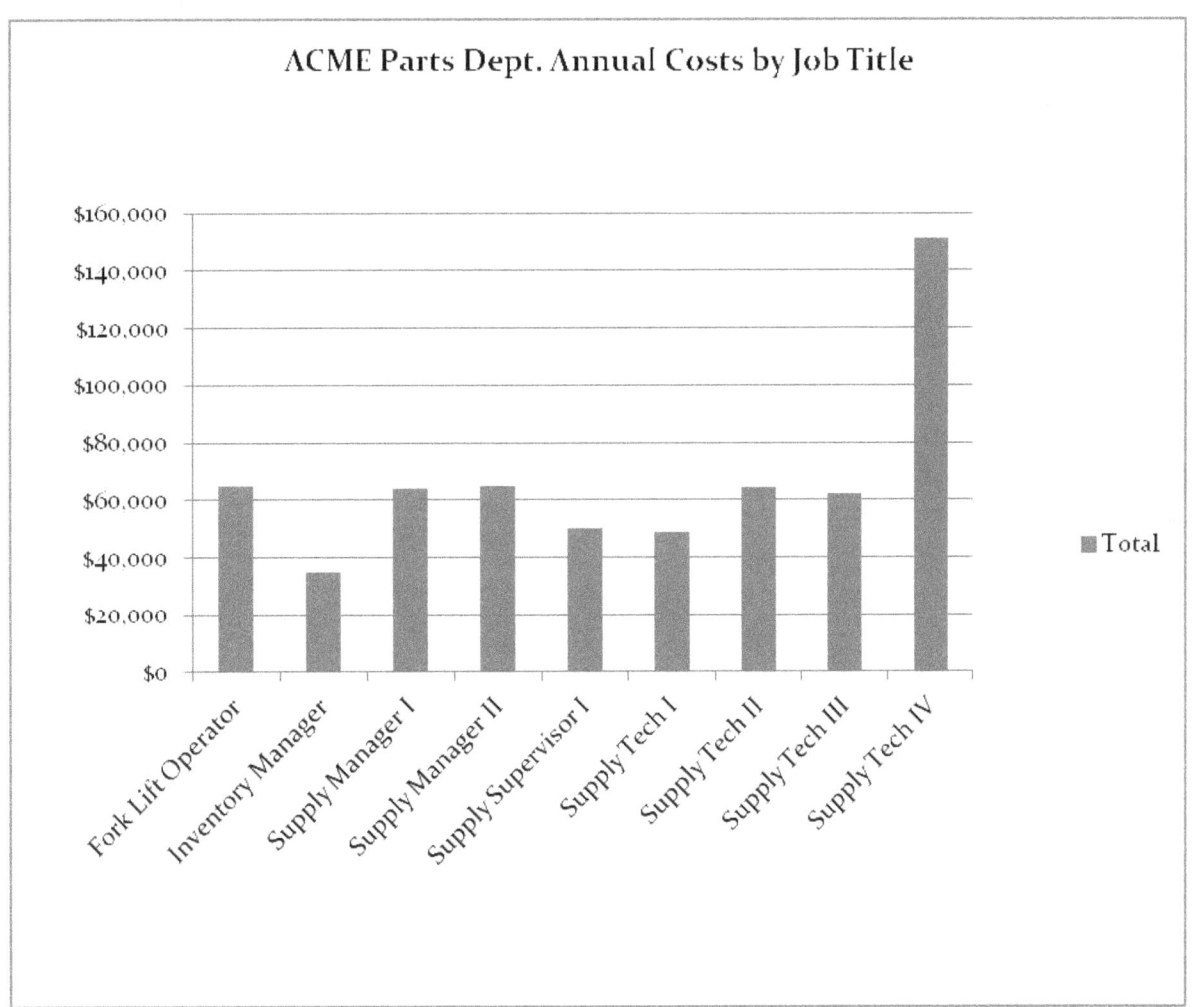

Figure 7-7 PivotChart – ACME Parts Department annual costs by job title.

Satisfied requirements for Chart 3: ACME Parts Dept Annual costs by Job title.

Charts and Graphs
Module 7

Chart 4 - Name and years of service of each employee in the ACME Parts Dept.

Finally, you will create Chart 4. First, you will consider what question are you being asked, to answer? The ACME Parts Director, asked for a chart that shows Employees (last and first name) by Job title and years of service.

Populating PivotTable Field List to create a PivotChart

So, to answer the question, you need the "Last Name", "First Name" and "Job Title". These fields will be placed in the Axis Fields box. The "Years of Service" field will be used to summarize your answer. It should be placed in the Values box. See Figure 7-8.

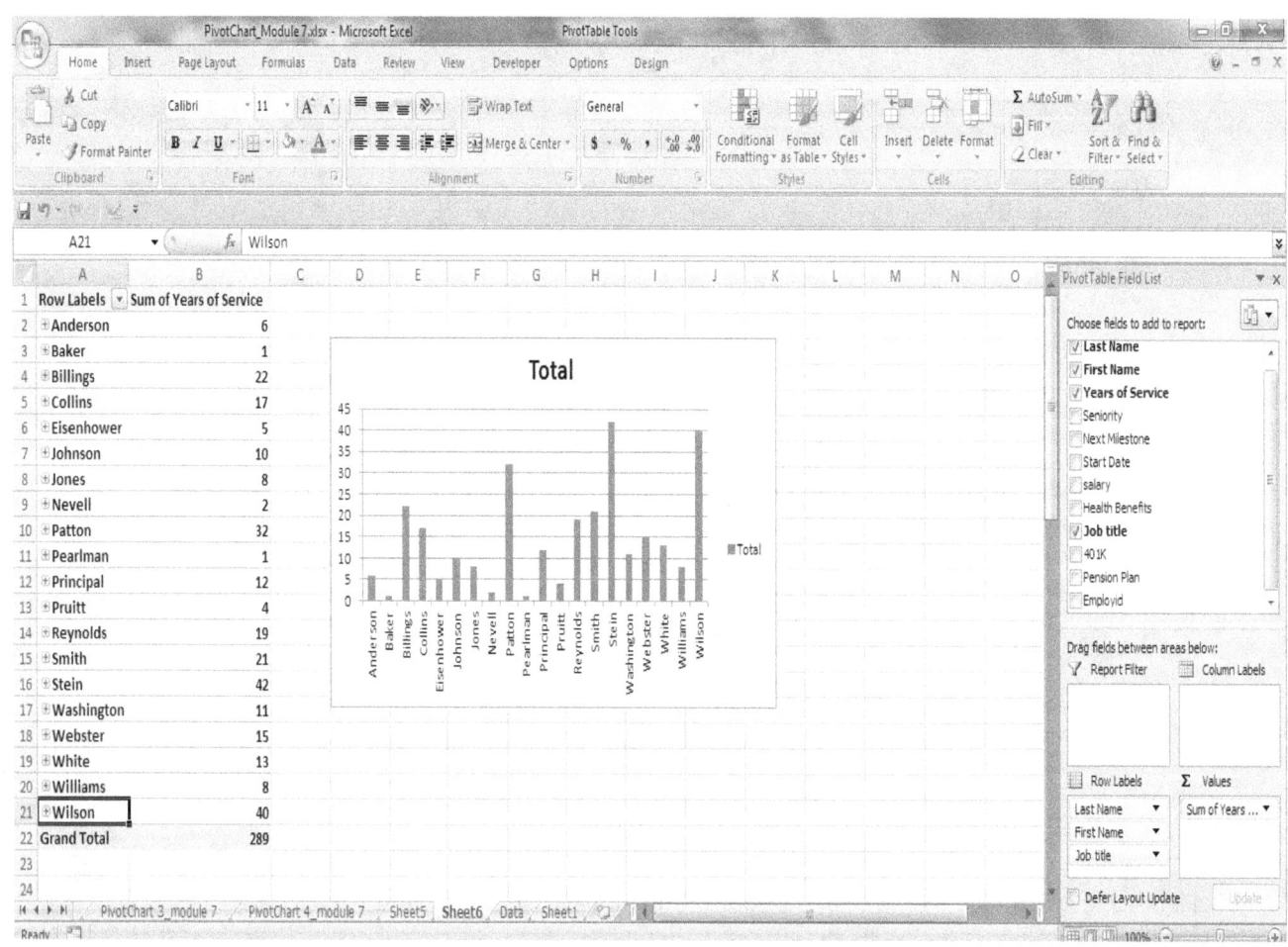

Figure 7-8 PivotTable– Name and years of service of each employee in ACME Parts Dept.

Adding a Title Name to Chart 4 - Name and years of service of each employee in the ACME Parts Dept.

Now, to make your chart easy, for the executive to interpret, you will rename the title of this chart. This is accomplished by,

1) placing your cursor on the Title box, located at the top of your newly created chart.
2) Next, press your left mouse button once to access the title.
3) Next, type "ACME Parts Dept. Employees by Name , Title and Years of Service".
4) Now, select the "Layout" tab from the Ribbon Interface.
5) Select, the "Axes" icon from the "Axes group".
6) Select, "Primary Horizontal Axis title" then select from the pop-up menu, "None".
7) Next, select, the "Axis title" icon from the "Labels group".
8) Select, "Primary Horizontal Axis title", then select, from the pop-up menu , "Title Below Axis". *A text box will appear, below your horizontal axis*.
10) Type "Salary" in the Axis text box.
11) Next, select the "Axis title" icon from the "Labels group"
12) Select, "Primary Vertical Axis title" then select from the pop-up menu, "Rotated Title". *A rotated text box will appear next to your vertical axis*.
13) Type "US Currency" in the Axis text box.

Chart 4 - Name, Title and years of service of each employee in the ACME Parts Dept.

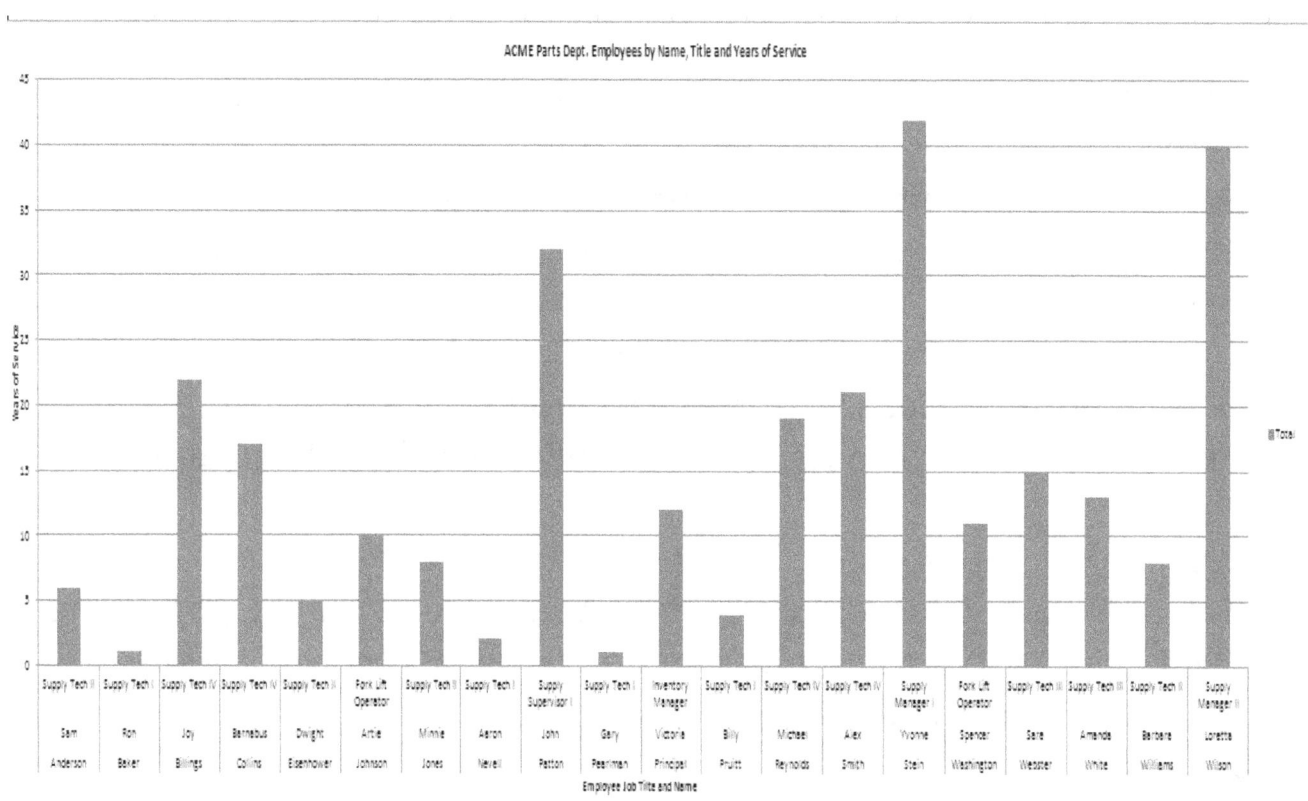

Figure 7-9 PivotChart – Name, Title and years of service of each employee in ACME Parts Dept.

Satisfied requirements for Chart 4: Job title and Years of service of each employee in the ACME Parts Department.

What have you learned so far?

1) What is a PivotChart.
2) How to identify the question to answer before you create a PivotChart.
3) How to create PivotCharts from a PivotTable, using functions located in the Insert tab.
4) How to access the PivotChart Filter pane.
5) How to interpret the data populated in the Field List, Row Labels, Column Labels and Values boxes, within the PivotChart Filter pane.
6) How to create a PivotChart.

FORMATTING AND THEMES
LOOKS ARE EVERYTHING

Formatting and Themes

Module 8

Scenario 8 : Its now time to put the final touches on your work. The job is not complete until you add the window dressing. Therefore, in this module we will discuss adding formatting and themes to your tables and charts.

If you remember, at the end of the "Create Data table" lesson, in module 5, you discovered the "Design" tab. You will now revisit the "Design" tab. To remember where we left off, access the original data table you created. It should look like the one shown below.

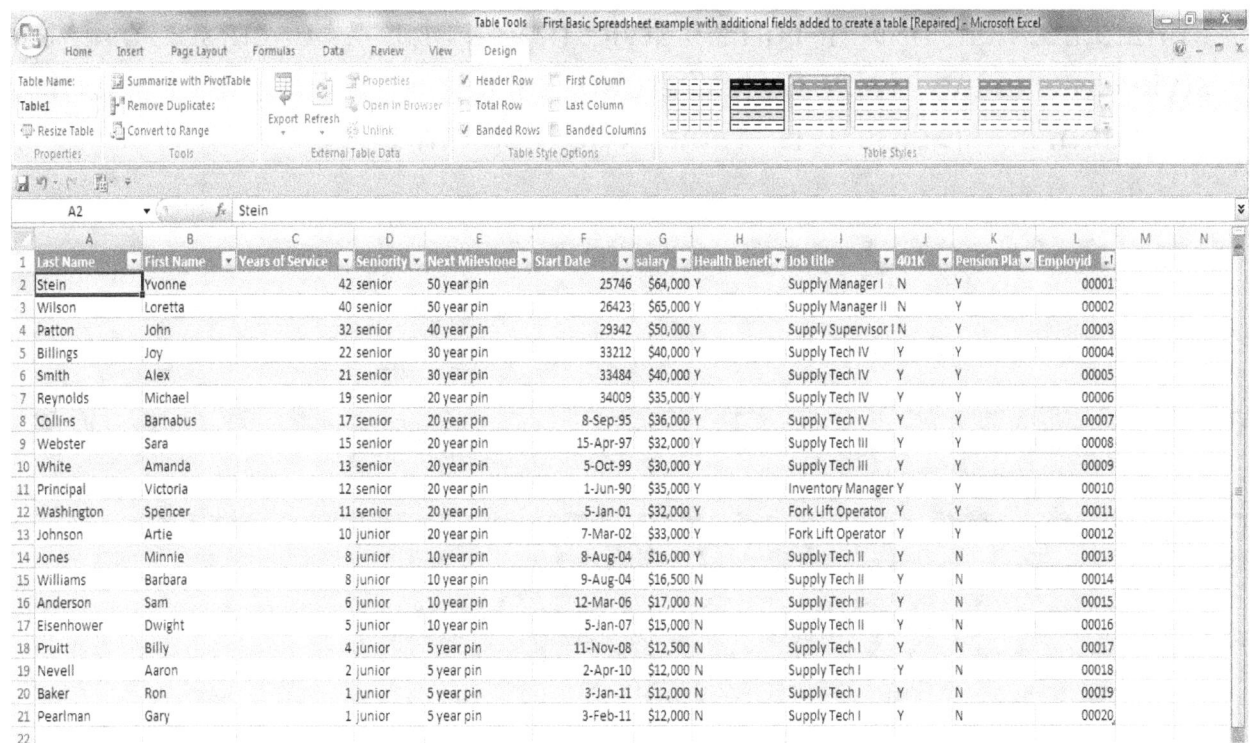

Figure 8-1 Ms Excel 2007 Data Table.

*Access the **"Formatting and Themes_module8.xlsx"** from the CD that came with this manual to see hands-on examples, Original_DTable_Module 8; Med17_Dtable_Module 8; Equity Theme_Module 8 ; Chart4_Equity Theme_Module 8 ; Chart4_withbkgrd_Module 8; and Cover.*

Designing Styles in your Data Table

1. Place your cursor on any field in your data table. Click the left mouse button once. The "Design" tab will appear in the Ribbon Interface.
2. Select the "Design" tab.
3. Look at the "Table Style Options" group.
4. As you can see (fig. 8-2), the "Header Row" and "Banded Rows" check boxes are selected. That is the reason why your data table displays a header row, and why the row colors alternate between grey and white.
5. Now, from within the "Table Styles" group, select the style to the immediate right of your current style. (if you place your cursor, over the style icons in the "Table Styles" group, it'll display the name of your new selection. In this case, it is "Table Style Medium 17".

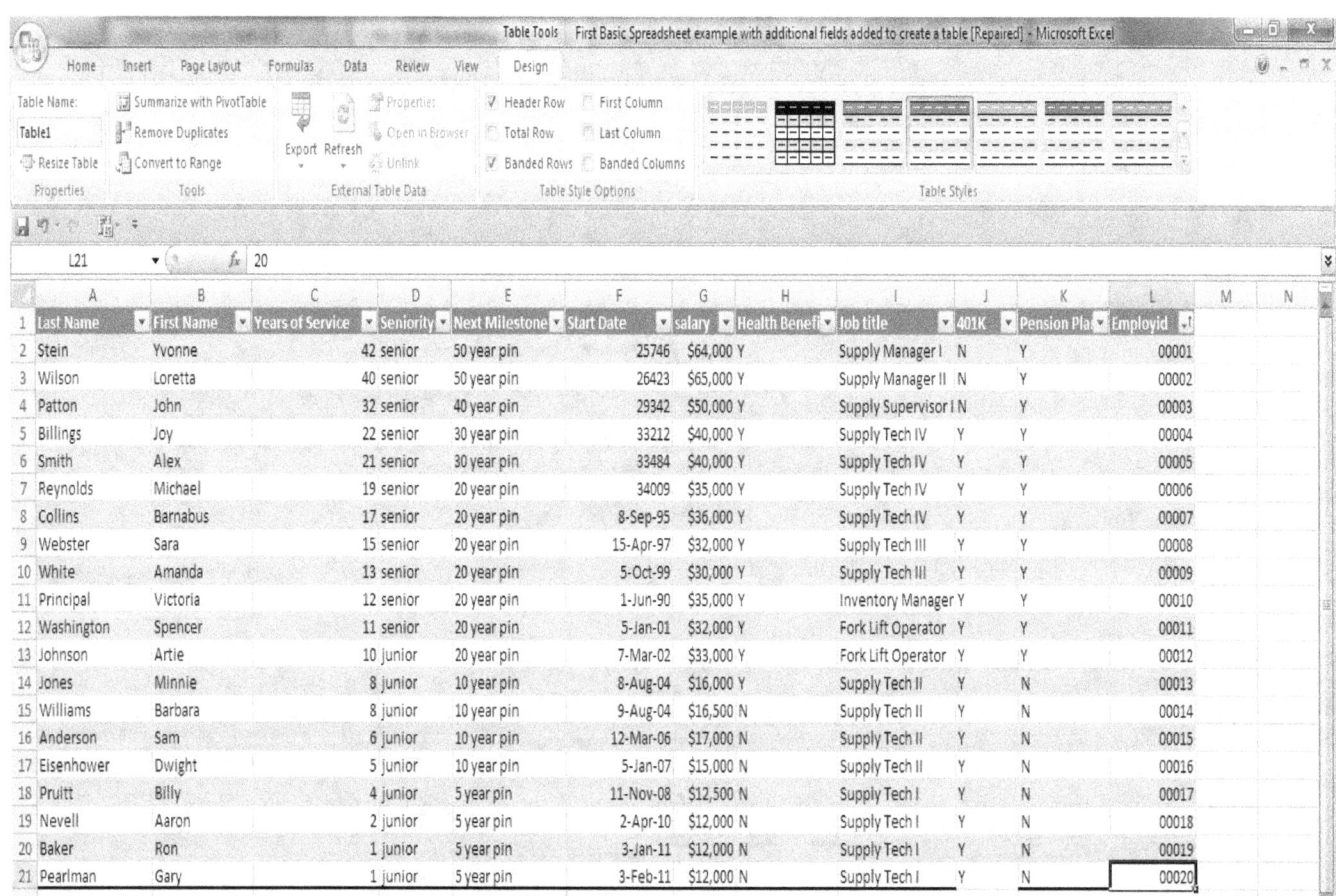

Figure 8-2 Data table formatted to display Table Style Medium 17.

Formatting and Themes

Module 8

Adding a theme to your Data Table

Next, you will add a theme to your data table. A document theme is a set of formatting choices that include, a set of theme colors; theme fonts (including heading and body text fonts); and theme effects (including lines and fill effects).

So add a Theme.
1. Go to the "Page Layout" tab.
2. Select the "Themes" icon from the "Themes" group.
3. Select the "Equity" theme from the "Themes" drop-down menu.
Figure 8-3, displays the data table with an Equity Theme.

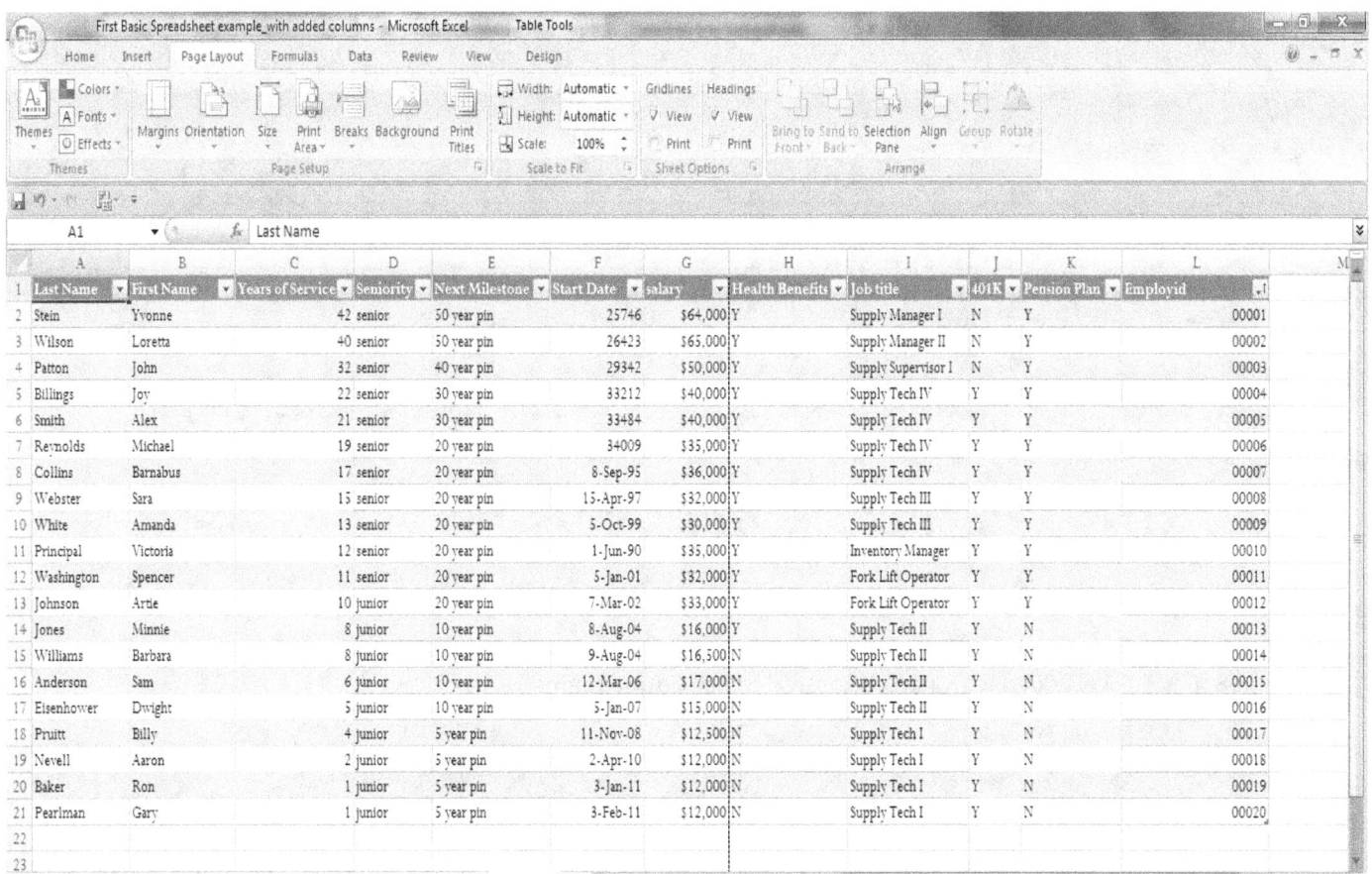

Figure 8-3 Data table formatted to display the Equity theme.

103

Next, lets take a look at Chart 4 and add a theme to it. Open Chart4 - Name and Years of service of each employee in the ACME Parts Dept.

As you can see (figure 8-4), your bar chart in Chart 4 has also changed to the Equity theme. It reflects the same font and color as your data table.

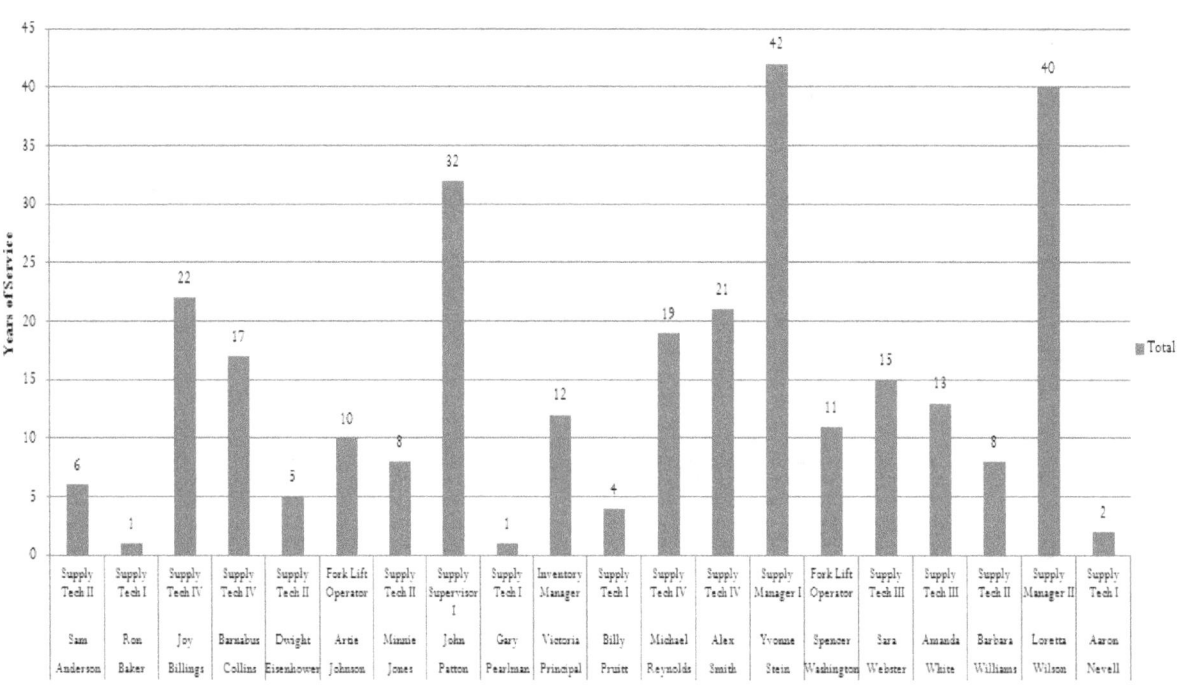

Figure 8-4 MS Excel 2007 PivotChart formatted to use Equity theme.

Now that you are comfortable with managing data within Excel, lets try to impress. Lets add a background to your chart. Since ACME is a Parts Department, you will select a vehicle parts picture as your background (See Figure 8-5) .

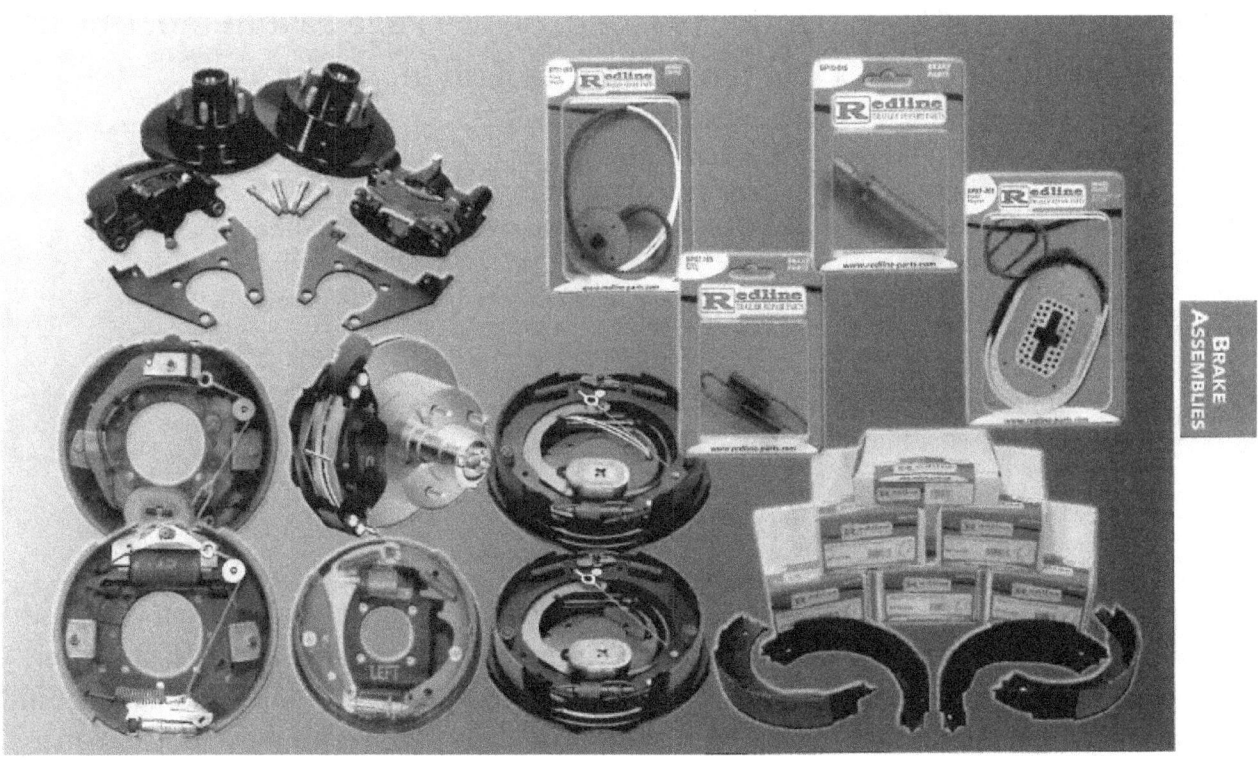

Figure 8-5 Auto parts picture to be used as background on a MS Excel 2007 worksheet.

Formatting and Themes
Module 8

Adding a background to a chart.

While still keeping Chart 4's bar chart open,

1) go to the Page Layout tab.
2) Within the "Page Setup" group of the "Page Layout" tab, select the "Background" icon. This will take you to the Pictures Library, on your hard drive, where jpg (picture) files are stored.
3) Since ACME is a Parts Department, you will select the "Brake_Assemblies_2. jpg" file as your background.
4) Now go to the "Sheet Options" group, on the Page Layout tab. Uncheck the "View" check box located under the Gridlines column.

Congratulations, you have just added a background to your chart. See Figure 8-6.

Important note: The background picture is for display only. It will not print. If you desire to print your chart or spreadsheet, with a background picture, you must 1) Select "Insert" tab, 2) go to "Text " group, 3) select "Header & Footer" icon, 4) select "Custom Header " button, 5) place your cursor in the "Center Section" box, and press the left mouse button once. 6) Select the 'Insert Picture" icon   .

7) This will take you to the Pictures Library, 8) Select Brake_Assemblies_2, 9) Select "OK" button. 10) Congratulations, your background will print with your chart.

Formatting and Themes
Module 8

PivotChart with added background picture.

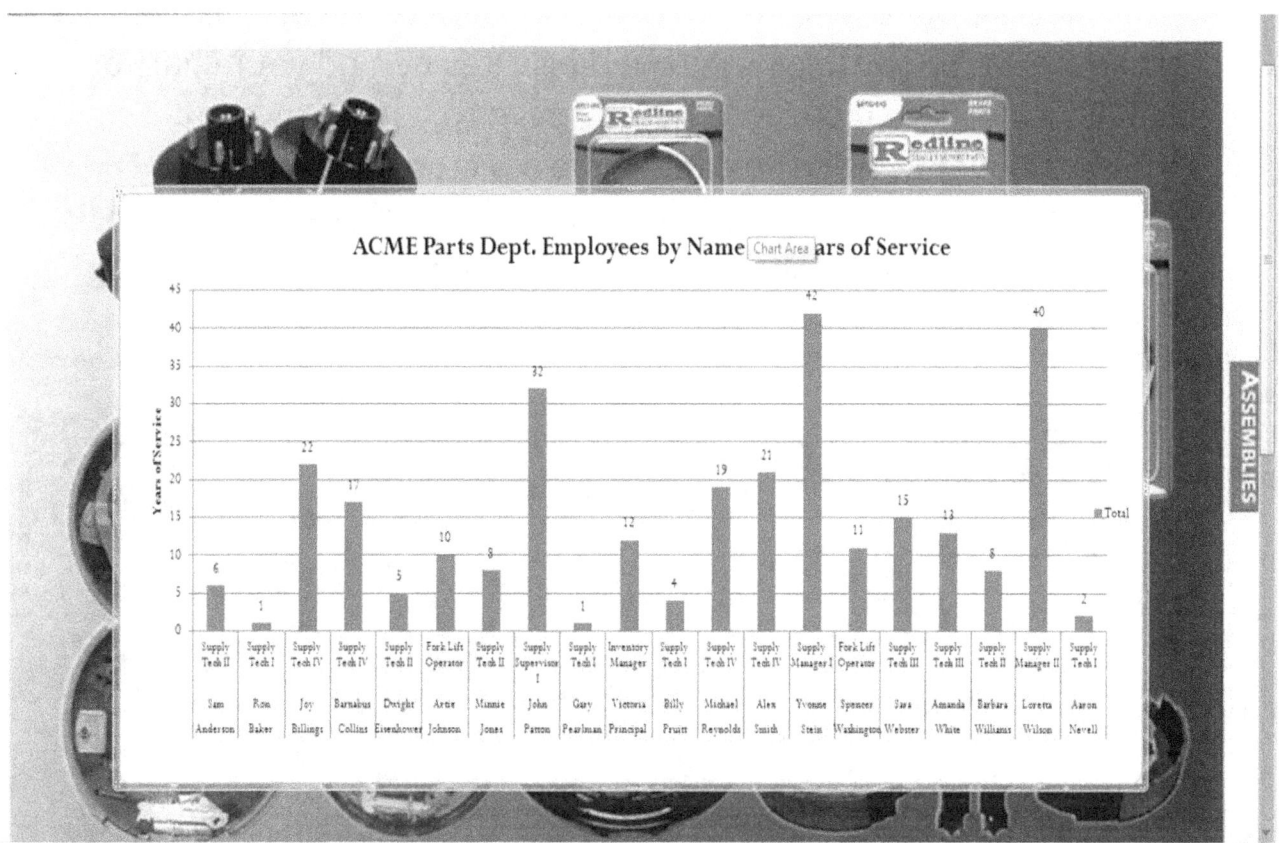

Figure 8-6 MS Excel 2007 PivotChart with Auto parts picture shown as background

Creating a picture as a cover page.

Sometimes background pictures on charts or data tables are distracting. So, an alternative to putting background pictures behind your chart or data would be to use a picture as a cover page to your workbook. To accomplish this, you would copy and paste a picture on an empty worksheet. Next, name the worksheet "cover sheet" (see, circled tab, in figure 8-7). This cover worksheet would be in front of your data table worksheet, as shown below.

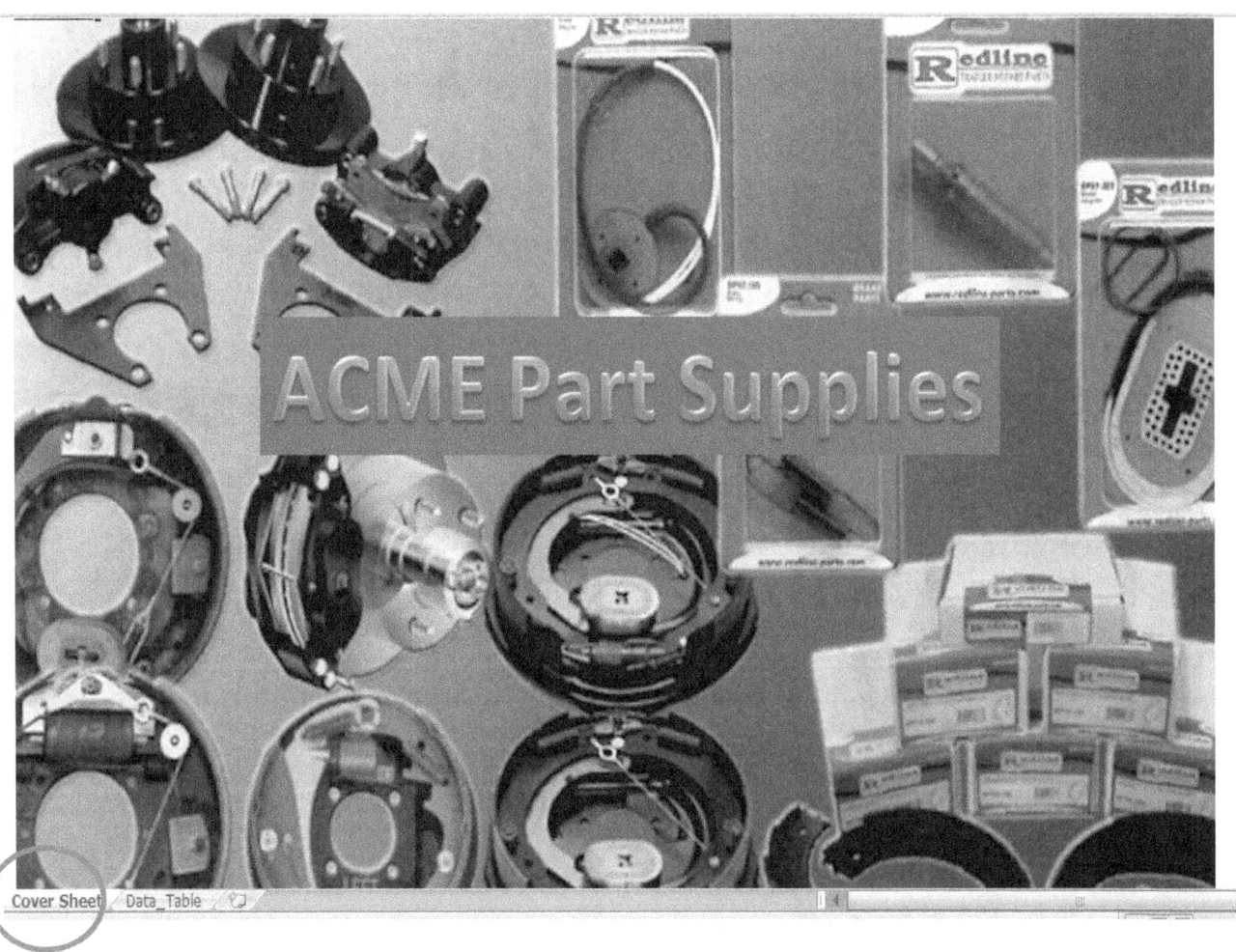

Figure 8-7 Auto parts picture used as background for a workbook cover sheet.

What have you learned so far?

1) How to access the Design tab.
2) How to add a header with color fill to your Data Table.
3) How to add banded color rows, to your Data Table.
4) How to access, the Page Layout tab.
5) How to add a theme to your Data Table.
6) How to add a picture background to your workbook.

PRINTING THE FINISHED PRODUCT

Printing
Module 9

You have arrived at the finish line. All that remains, is to create a hardcopy of your report. Since you have put so much work into creating your presentation, you may want to make sure anyone reviewing it can properly navigate it.

Adding navigation information to your finished document.

Navigation information needs to be added to your document.
Our definition of navigation information is page numbers, dates, and titles, to name a few. This type of information will inform anyone referencing your workbook about the version (date), filename, page title and page number.

In order for you to add navigation information to your Data Table you will use the "Insert" and "Design" tabs.
1) Select "Insert" tab.
2) Go to "Text " group.
3) Select "Header & Footer" icon.
4) Notice you are now in the "Design" tab.
5) Go to the "Header and Footer Elements" group.
   As you can see, there are several functions, to choose from, in this group.

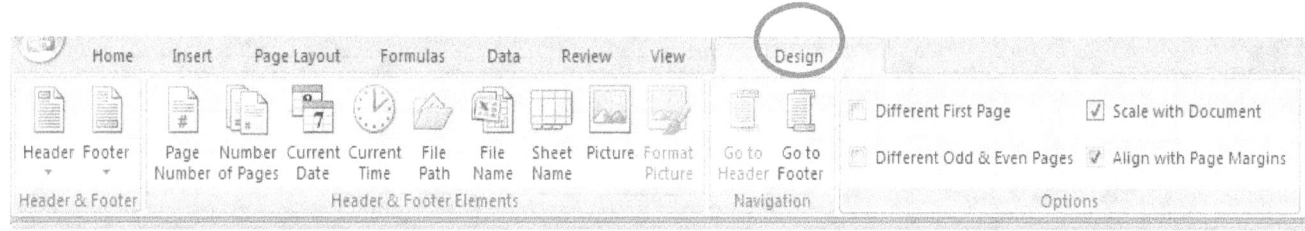

Figure 9-1 MS Excel 2007 Ribbon Interface "Design" tab.

6) Before we discuss each function, select "Sheet Name". As you will see, the name you created on the Data Table's sheet tab will appear in the header of your document.
7) Now, select the Navigation group on the "Design" tab. Select "Go to Footer". Go to the "Header & Footer Elements" group, then select, "Page Number".

111

Printing
Module 9

Creating a header title by using the MS Excel "Sheet Name".

Selection of the "Sheet Name" function, adds the sheet tab name to the header title of your document. Selecting the "Page Number" function, places a page number in the footer of your document.

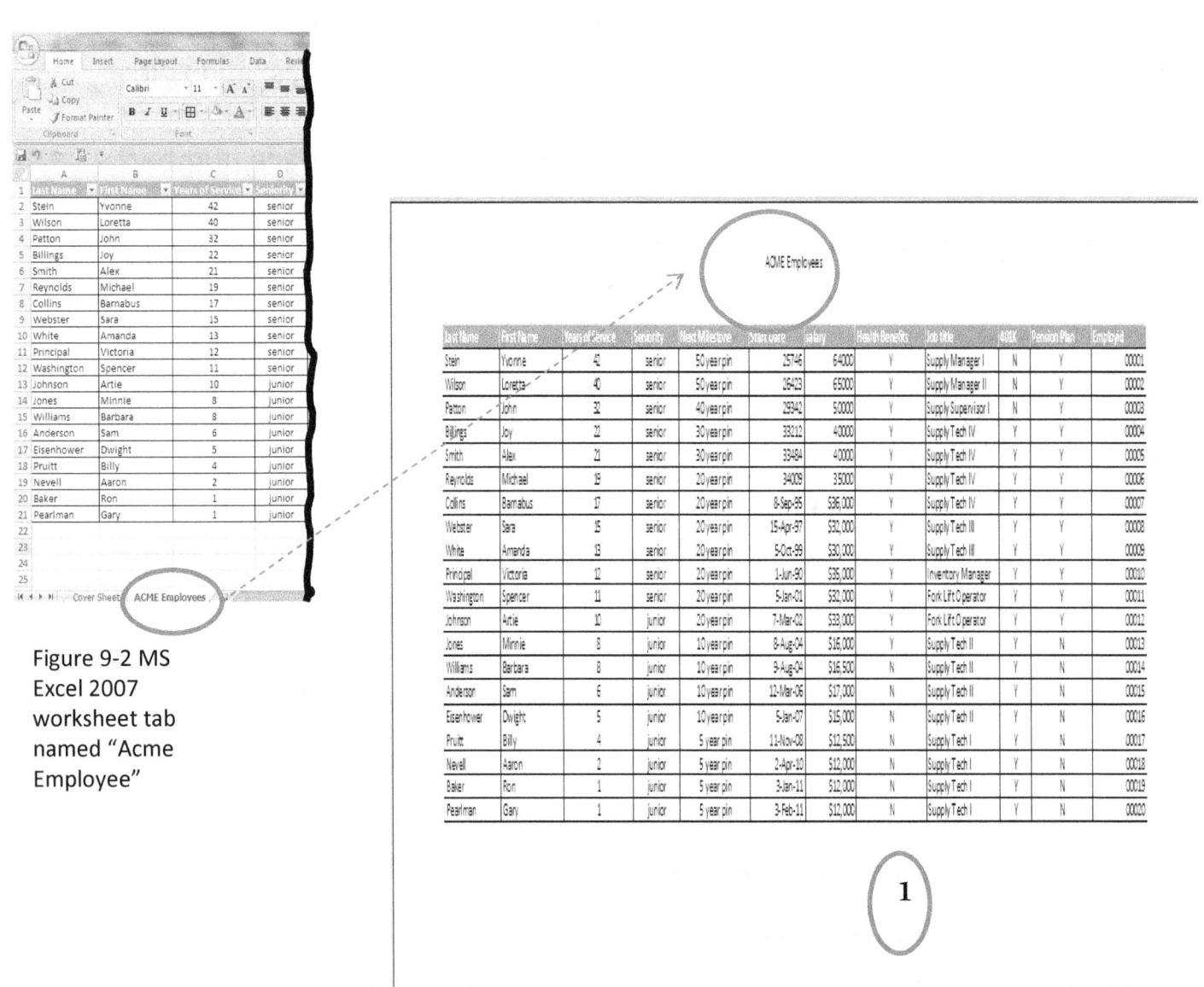

Figure 9-2 MS Excel 2007 worksheet tab named "Acme Employee"

Figure 9-3 MS Excel 2007 worksheet with tab name added to header title and page number added to footer.

Header & Footer functions descriptions.

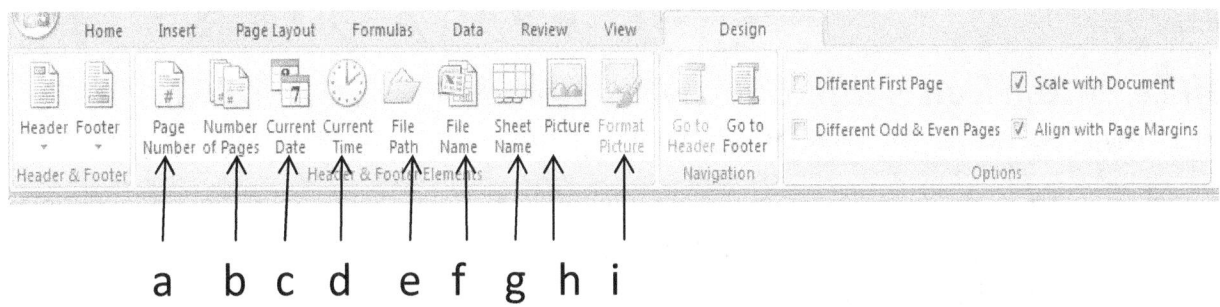

Figure 9-4 MS Excel 2007 Ribbon Interface "Design" tab.

a) **Page Number** - adds a page number, to the header or footer area, of your
worksheet.
b) **Number of Pages** – adds to header or footer, the total pages, that the selected worksheet, covers.
c) **Current Date** – adds to header or footer, the current date, to the selected worksheet.
d) **Current Time** – adds to header or footer, the current time, to the selected worksheet.
e) **File Name** - adds to header or footer, the file name, to the selected worksheet.
f) **File Path** – adds to header or footer, the full path, of where this workbook was saved, on your computer.
g) **Sheet Name** - adds to header or footer, the tab name.
h) **Picture** – adds to header or footer, a picture.
i) **Format Picture** – adds to header or footer, the Format, of the picture. You can change the brightness, contrast, or size.

Now that you have added Navigation Information to your document, all that is left is to save and print your document.

So, you have come full circle. The Print function is located where you started, under the Office Button Icon.

The **Office Button Icon** is where you will go to finish your Excel adventure. As you should remember, the **Office Button Icon** menu is divided into 3 sections.

We informally called these sections:
1) File Handling (create, open or save)
2) File Print and Publish (print, prepare, send and publish)
3) File Close (exit)

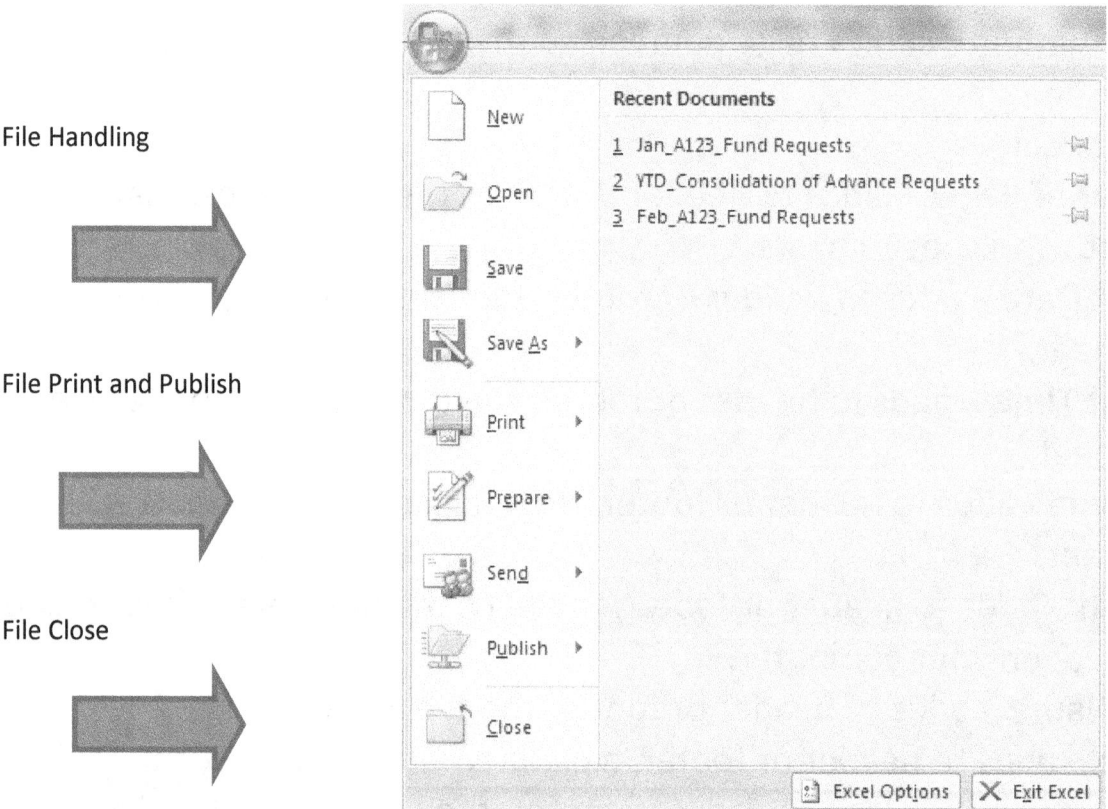

Figure 9-5 Office Button menu file management commands.

Saving your MS Excel document.

1) To save a copy of your work you will first go to the File Handling section.
2) Within the File Handling (create, open or save) section, you will select the **Save** icon. This will save a copy of your spreadsheet to your hard drive.

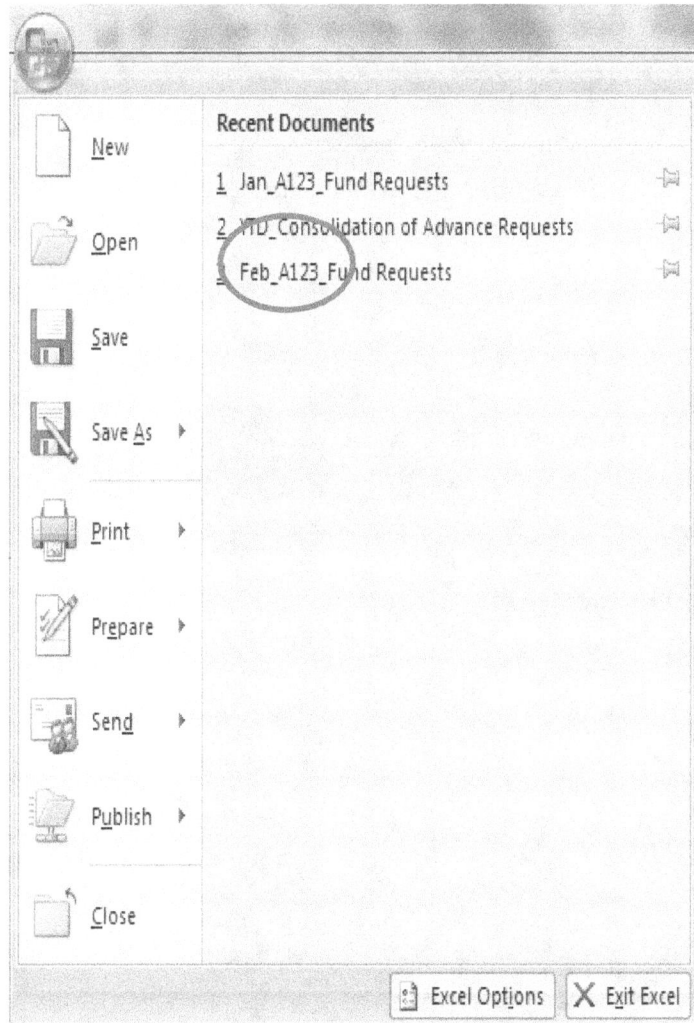

Figure 9-6 Office Button menu file management commands, File Handling section

Printing

Module 9

You have now saved a copy of your work. Next, you will select "Print" from the Office Button Icon's, "File Print and Publish" section.

File Print and Publish

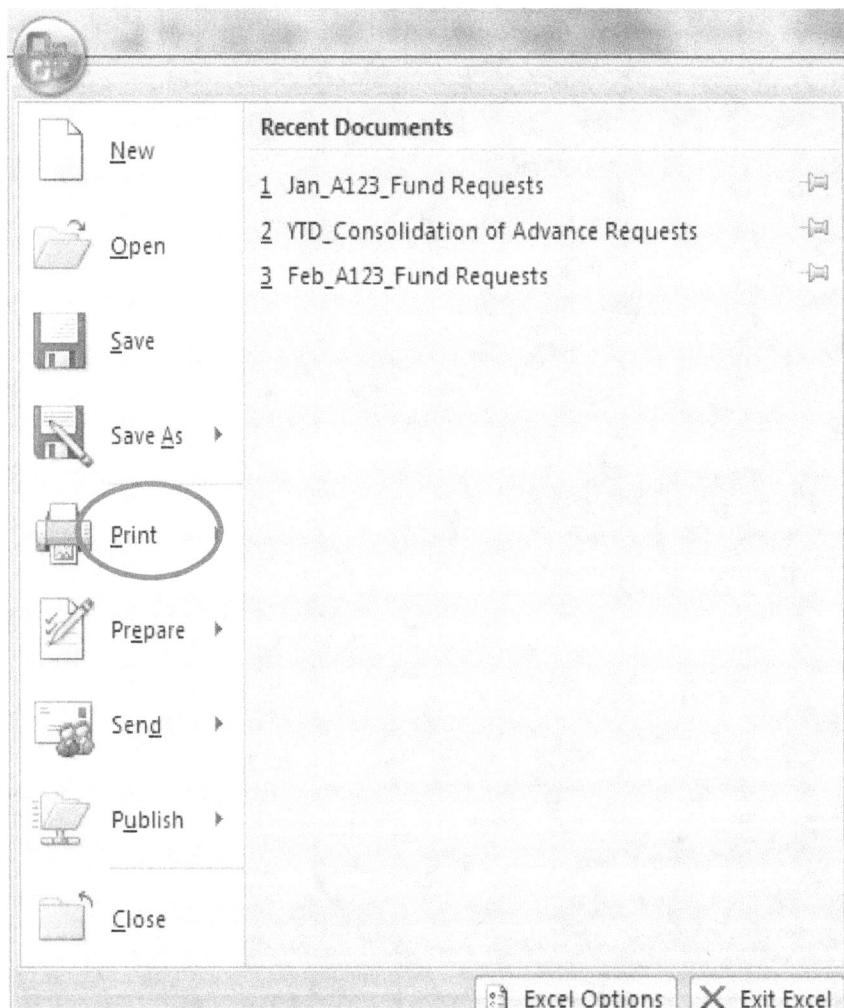

Figure 9-7 Office Button menu file management commands, File Print and Publish section.

Printing
Module 9

Printing your Excel document.

Upon selecting "Print", you will be presented with a print menu. This menu will show the name of the Printer which will receive your document. Select, "OK", located on the bottom right, of the Print menu.

Congratulations, you can now pick up your report from the selected printer.

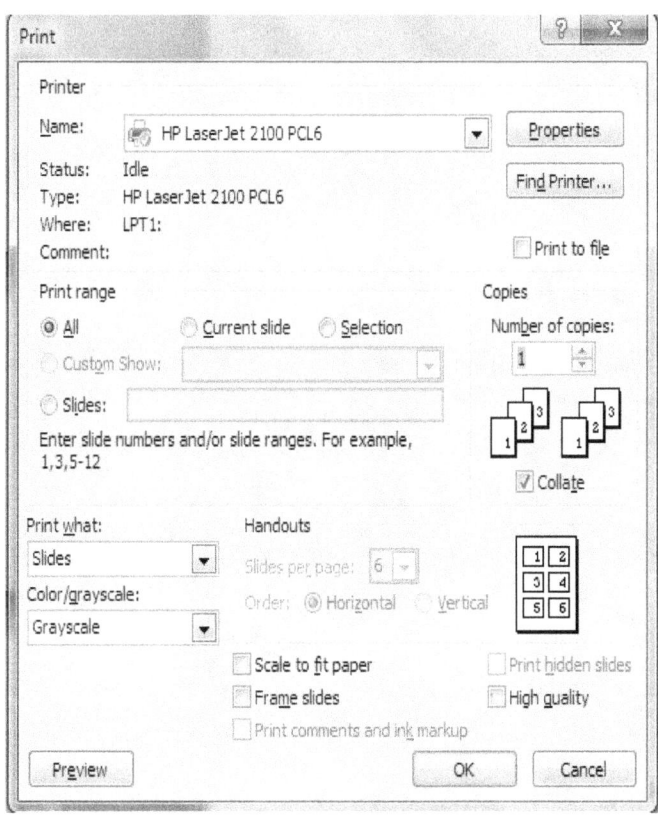

Figure 9-8 MS Excel 2007 Print menu.

Printing

Module 9

You are almost done. The final step is to select "Close" from the "File Close" section.

File Close

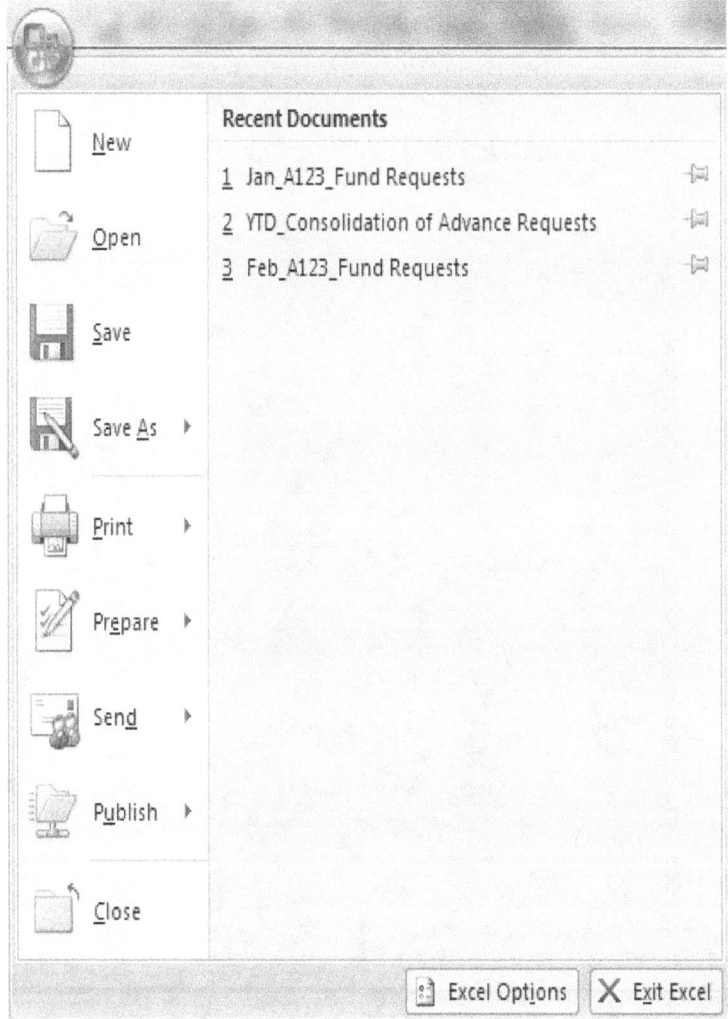

Figure 9-9 Office Button menu file management commands, File Close section.

Exit your MS Excel document.

The "Close" icon will allow you to properly exit your new or updated spreadsheet. When you are done working on your spreadsheet, choosing the "Close" icon will cause Excel to display a prompt menu. The prompt will ask, "Do you want to save changes you made...?" (Figure 9-10). This prompt menu will remind you to save all updates made to your spreadsheet. It is a good practice, to always select the "Close" icon before shutting down.

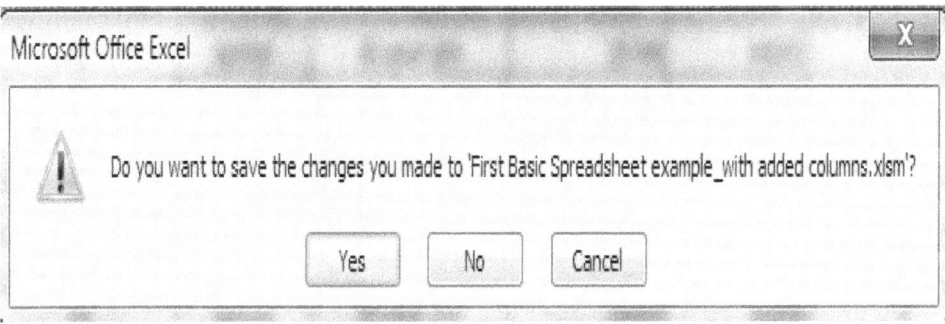

Figure 9-10 MS Office Excel 2007 prompt.

What have you learned so far?

1) How to add navigation information to your document using the "Insert" and "Design" tabs.
2) The definition of header and footer icon's functions.
3) How to Save, Print, and Exit a workbook by using the functions within the Office Button Icon.

Thank you for your time and attention.
Good luck with your use of the Excel tool.

To order a replacement, for a lost CD, or to request on-site classroom training go to TopToolsandTraining.com

No part of this publication may be reproduced, transmitted, translated or stored without the express written permission of the publisher. Created and printed in the United States of America.